DISCIPLEMAKING
Doing What Christ Commanded

BY
JUDY STREETER

Bloomington, IN Milton Keynes, UK
authorHOUSE

AuthorHouse™ *AuthorHouse*™ *UK Ltd.*
1663 Liberty Drive, Suite 200 *500 Avebury Boulevard*
Bloomington, IN 47403 *Central Milton Keynes, MK9 2BE*
www.authorhouse.com *www.authorhouse.co.uk*
Phone: 1-800-839-8640 *Phone: 08001974150*

© 2006 Zionsville Fellowship. All rights reserved.

No part of this book may be reproduced, stored in a retrieval system, or transmitted by any means without the written permission of the author.

First published by AuthorHouse 2/13/2006

ISBN: 1-4259-1816-6 (sc)

Printed in the United States of America
Bloomington, Indiana

This book is printed on acid-free paper.

To Tom,

My affable theologian in residence

who truly understands what it means

to nourish and cherish

Contents

	INTRODUCTION	IX
	PREFACE - A NEW BEGINNING	XV
I	THE OVERARCHING CALL	1
II	HEEDING THE COMMISSION	6
III	SCRIPTURAL PORTRAYAL	11
IV	DEFINING THE TERM	17
V	INTERNAL MOTIVATION	24
VI	EXTERNAL MOTIVATION	32
VII	EQUIPPING THE EQUIPPERS	40
VIII	ONE-ON-ONE VERSUS GROUP DISCIPLESHIP	48
IX	THE SELECTION PROCESS	56
X	REPRODUCTION	66
XI	KEEPING THE BIGGER PICTURE IN MIND	75
XII	THE WOMAN DISCIPLER	83
XIII	FINAL THOUGHTS	96
	APPENDIX - THE CURRICULUM	107

INTRODUCTION

I was a busy wife and mother of three children ages 3, 5 and 7 when I participated in one of Judy Streeter's first discipleship groups in Indiana. The material was stimulating, challenging and practical, just what I needed to stir my macaroni and cheese brain. Our discipleship group met for one year. Little did I know the countless number of times I would refer to the reading material, replay lively discussions in my head, and even recall casual asides from Judy in the years to come. That discipleship group was a fundamental building block in my walk with Christ, my marriage and my family.

Now, Judy has honed the material even more and offers it in "Disciplemaking: Doing What Christ Commanded." The book is a work of excellence, which isn't surprising to any one who knows Judy. She has a well-earned reputation for being on target. As a result, the book is incisive, thought-provoking and above all, challenges readers to know God and to examine their relationship with God. "Disciplemaking: Doing What Christ Commanded" is a much-needed resource in a world of casual Christianity.

Lori Nye

As a young believer in Christ in 1986, I had the blessing of being in a discipleship group led by Judy Streeter. The material that was covered gave me a firm spiritual foundation, a solid understanding of Biblical Truth and a much greater knowledge of the God in whom I had put my faith. I learned to love God with my mind as well as my heart.

I know it is Judy's conviction that in our post-Christian culture, believers must be grounded in a solid knowledge of Biblical truth and doctrine so as not to be swayed by the many subtle, and not so subtle, forms of spirituality and secularist philosophies so prevalent today.

I am grateful that God has given Judy the vision and desire to equip women so that they can, in turn, equip others. It is wonderful to see the wisdom she has gained through many years of experience finally put in written form to help others answer God's charge to us to "go and make disciples."

Viki LaChapelle

Praise God for Judy Streeter and her obedience to Jesus Christ in heeding the Great Commission to "go and make disciples." Through reading, meditating, memorizing and discussing the Word of God in a women's group, the foundation for my walk with Jesus Christ was established. Further reading and dialogues gave me a greater understanding of the family, prayer, the church, the culture, witnessing, and church history.

Discipling others has been an opportunity for continual study and prayer, so that my mind be enlightened, my heart enflamed and my life transformed to equip other women to, in turn, "go and make disciples."

The fire has been ignited for life-long learning and the importance of passing it on to the next generation. Thank you, Judy, for discipling me in 1985-86.

Roberta Parks

Like many whose walk with the Lord began as an adult, I spent the first few years in weekly Bible studies. While these studies contributed to my knowledge of Scripture and deeper convictions, something was missing. I longed to develop the ability to better defend the truth and apply it to every aspect of life and thought. On my own, this proved to be quite a challenge.

At just the right time, I was blessed with the experience of being discipled by Judy. It was in the context of this committed relationship that I was challenged to think more critically about the essential truths of our faith, articulate them more clearly, defend them more confidently, and exercise them more faithfully. More than any other woman in my life, Judy has nurtured my growth as a follower of Christ. During those weekly meetings and for years since then, she has faithfully led me by her example. Her tireless commitment to nurturing and equipping others had produced much fruit, including the pages that follow. I trust that the wisdom and experience permeating this book will challenge and inspire you to do the same.

Susan Albers

How excited I am to see Judy Streeter's discipleship manual finally in print so that others can learn from it and implement its contents to disciple others. I was personally discipled by Judy in 1988-1990. Though I had been a Christian for a few years, the hours we spent together weekly as a group of five women helped to solidify what I believed, why I believed it and how to defend my beliefs in an intelligible way. I kept all my materials in a notebook, and to this day, I still pull from its contents. I like to think of discipleship as a river from which my main growth as a Christian came.

Now, I may delve into other tributaries of ministry, but I always draw from the well of the original body of water from which I grew and was nourished. I know of no one who has a heart for discipleship as Judy does. How thankful I am that she has chosen to publish her much used, tried and true materials for discipleship.

Patty Blakley

The practice of discipleship is a position of both a learner and as a learner-leader. When we become Jesus' disciples, He calls us to learn of Him and also to lead others to learn of Him. When Judy led me and three other women according to the practice of this book, I closely examined the content of my faith in an environment of intellectual integrity, rich content, cultural awareness and healthy relationship.

Since that time, I have replicated her pattern in four groups of different ages. Judy articulates a motivation and pattern that is spiritually and relationally healthy and can be replicated successfully and flexibly. Her experience paves the way. This pattern better equips me to do what was commanded by Jesus in both learning of Him and leading others to be learners of Him. Her investment in me is incalculable until we reach heaven.

Becky Moreland

Jesus' words to His chosen men were poignant and clear: "Go and make disciples of all nations…teaching them to obey everything I have commanded you…" (Matthew 28:19, 20). The words of Paul to Timothy were compelling: "And the things you have heard me say in the presence of many witnesses entrust to reliable men who will also be qualified to teach others" (II Timothy 2:2).

In this book, Judy Streeter gives both clarity and inspiration to the whole idea of discipleship. Born out of her years of experience in teaching, mentoring, nurturing, guiding and discipling women, these pages contain a deep well of resources for those who take the call of the Great Commission seriously. It resonates with the truth of Scripture, prompting women to be "kingdom minded" and to be faithful laborers in the harvest. Judy's insight gives readers a vision for God's plan of passing the baton of truth. She identifies the very personal nature of discipleship and provides a foundation for effective leadership.

Discipleship has been a priority in Judy's life for over 30 years. A commitment to and a deep love for her Lord, a devoted and fervent prayer life, a humble and teachable spirit and a servant's heart are the marks of this woman's character. The legacy of her faithful obedience to God's call is immeasurable. My mind and heart have received from this gifted teacher, and it is with joy and zeal that I commend this book to any woman who desires to take Jesus at His word and do the work for the glory of God!

Tana Henry

PREFACE

A NEW BEGINNING

In 1972, I was 29 years old and my children were ages six and three. It was a year of dramatic change for us as Tom and I left the familiar "traditional" evangelical church in order to discover and practice "church" in a new and fresh way. Not a hasty decision, but rather one that seemed to be the next step in a pursuit for authentic church life, this involved several years of an industrious study of church history, engagement with the post-60's culture, and participation in small group Bible studies (which were unique at that time). About 50 of us met on Sunday mornings in rented facilities, which shifted the emphasis on church buildings to our home. During the week, our home was a gathering place for the body of Christ, and that change alone clarified a pure definition of the church…that it truly was "people" (not a building), those "called out," and that we were a living organism. Without the trappings of endless church busyness, committees, programs, buildings, promotional gimmicks and other energy-sapping activities, we were experiencing a simplicity and beauty in church life we had never known.

We loved the church of Jesus Christ and desired to see substantial spiritual and personal growth in the lives of people. We quickly learned there were others who were desirous of the same thing so our little group grew steadily and within two years, we were dealing with more than 300 people. A church such as this naturally attracted younger people, many of whom were "leftovers" from the 60's and

Vietnam and didn't feel accepted in conventional churches. Our dialogues were vigorous and productive, with many coming to faith in Christ.

Two major realities became obvious in my life (and I see them so much more clearly now than I did then):

- ✧ For the first time in my entire church experience, which was all of my life, I was surrounded by first-generation Christians. Many of these people had no Christian upbringing, no Christian jargon, no Christian mind, and very little knowledge of Biblical content.

- ✧ I was the "older woman." At age 29, I was the older example and model of the Titus II woman. This realization grew on me as I began to feel the pressure to spend time with many of these young women who were so desirous of growth in their new way of thinking and living.

I certainly didn't view myself as one who should be telling others how to grow. Part of that was because I had never been in a church where discipling one another was encouraged or practiced. No woman had ever approached me with the idea of mentoring or nurturing my growth, nor had I ever observed a regular ongoing ministry of discipleship, especially among women. So when the need was staring me in the face, I did not recognize it.

The other reason I was oblivious to my responsibility in discipling others was that I had always enjoyed active involvement in the music ministry of the church, and that was my identity and place of service. Really getting involved with people, their problems, struggles and personal development was foreign territory for me. Now, with minimal musical involvement, (as guitars became the primary instrument of the church in those days), I was forced to spend time with people, listen to them, and try to determine how they could be helped.

Only a few years separated me from these younger women, but we were a generation apart in thought and worldview. Most were victims of the 60's culture that had disillusioned them and left its scars. Having been raised in the conservative Bible belt of the Grand Rapids, Michigan area, I wasn't even close in understanding where they were coming from. I do not know if they particularly admired me, but I was there, available, and a woman who had known Christ all her life. They naturally assumed I would be able to guide them and were making overtures to that extent. One young woman asked me one day, "I don't really know what I need, but could I just sort of follow you around?"

I began a short-term summer Bible study with eight young women in a house where their children were being babysat in the basement during our study (and thus learning a practical lesson that it is better to have the little ones in a different place where their cries are not heard and responded to so frequently!). Using Titus 2:3-5, we took the character qualities mentioned and spent a week studying each one. It was an eye-opening experience as I learned firsthand that words like "good" were now relativistic terms, having lost the concrete definition they once had in my growing up years. As I became impacted with the thirst, hunger, cultural damage, yet potential of these young women, I realized that a nice little Bible study here and there was not going to cut it. In fact, Tom and I talked often in those days about the reality of our church becoming an ICU ward. Intensive care of people was necessary, to the point that our counseling load was more than we could bear. Much study and teaching was done on viewing the church as a community, and without the experience of us functioning as a *family* of believers, many of our people would never have been brought to health.

Tom was already getting together weekly with several men in the church for the purpose of disciplemaking and he encouraged me to begin meeting with their wives. It was difficult to limit myself to a few women because the need was so great, but I began with five. In uncharted waters, I developed material as we went along, trying to find a balance between the relational aspect of our meetings and the vertical (worship and study). Store-bought resources seemed unsatisfactory because they were either too elementary, cut-and-dried, or too need-specific. Quite frankly, there wasn't much available. I called several churches in the greater evangelical community in the Chicago area where we were living to ask what discipleship materials they were using only to learn that there was no "discipleship program" in any of the churches. Some parachurch organizations had materials for encouraging growth in new believers, and they were helpful in affirming what areas of study should be covered, but were not necessarily a good fit for long-term discipleship within the community of believers.

I smile (and cringe) when I think of those first groups I had in the mid-70's and sometimes wish I could do them over. Perhaps I was saved by the heavy relational emphasis of the day…that just getting together and loving each other satisfied part of the need. In fact, structure was protested in those days, so it was better to be flexible and exhibit genuine interest in the person rather than the material. It would have been most helpful and encouraging to have comrades who were also nurturing growth in other women, but even in the large evangelical circle we were acquainted with, this type of discipleship was absent. Becoming acutely aware of the need to teach younger women would sometimes invoke a cry of desperation from me, most often heard by Tom: "Where *are* all the 'older godly women,' and what are they doing?!"

There's no doubt that I was pushed into an area that is very clearly taught in Scripture. Not having a "discipleship mentality" even though raised in a Bible-teaching church, it took *really* getting involved with people to wake me up to the principles in Scripture I could even quote by memory. Something I do know for certain, if you are *really* involved with people, sooner or later you will face discipleship.

Judy Streeter

CHAPTER 1

THE OVERARCHING CALL

Inside the Buchenwald concentration camp at Weimer, Germany, where over 250,000 prisoners were confined between 1937-1945, and where the inscription on the main gate still reads, *JEDEM DAS SEINE,* ("To Each His Own"), there is a small area where tribute is paid to Dietrich Bonhoeffer. While standing there, one cannot help but speak softly when considering this man who was an impassioned follower of Christ, had a splendid career of theological scholarship in his future, but comprehended before others what National Socialism was going to do to Germany. Denouncing the corrupt political system, he chose to stay with his persecuted fellow Christians rather than escape to England, was arrested by the Gestapo and after months in several prison camps, including Buchenwald, was executed on April 9, 1945, just a few days before the Allied liberation.

In his classic book, *The Cost of Discipleship,* Bonhoeffer makes the statement, "When Christ calls a man, He bids him come and die." Although for Bonhoeffer it eventually meant physical death, in those words the essence of true discipleship is contained. Following Christ requires radical change. It involves leaving all and learning a new kind of belief, a new kind of trust and a new kind of faith. Bonhoeffer stressed that the essential unity of belief and obedience must be held together. *"Only he who believes is obedient and only he who is obedient believes."* Faith is only real when there is obedience, he says, and faith only becomes faith in the act of obedience.

When Christ issued His simple and cordial summons to His disciples to "Follow me," it was a call to follow a *person* and to submit to His absolute, direct authority. Their voluntary action of enlisting as His disciples forever distinguished them from the masses. After all, they had left everything to follow Christ. They had only Him.

Perhaps the disciples had an advantage in that they actually heard the voice of Jesus when He said, "Follow me." They recognized His bodily form and were given a clear directive from His very lips. The call wasn't to a clever concept, an exciting program or a seminar where they would receive a three-ringed binder full of ideas. There's no record that John, Andrew, Nathanael or Phillip wanted to see the syllabus first and check out the outline of material to be covered. The call was to a *person*...a relationship...it was a call to the authority of Jesus Christ. There was a physical parting with the old life in order to place themselves under the supremacy of this man not knowing where their surrender would take them. Immediately, obedience and submission were demonstrated and life was radically different.

I've pondered this scenario many times in considering the fact that we are first and foremost disciples of Christ, and those we teach must realize the same. Although we have not seen the bodily form or heard an audible voice, we believe the summons applies to us. The call is to follow a Person, to learn from His life and behavior, to imitate those character traits and humbly call Him Lord. Just how does the call of Christ apply to us today? If we answer that call, where will it lead us? What decisions and partings will it demand? How do we "leave all and follow Him?" How is a genuine "decision for Christ" demonstrated in today's modern world?

Certainly there is no way for us to identify with the experience of the original Twelve. The cost of their discipleship was incredibly high and we must stand in awe of their obedience. Throughout the ages, many have taken the call to follow Christ very seriously. These people have realized that grace itself is costly, not cheap. What cost God His Son cannot be cheap for us. Being "bought with a price" (I Cor. 6:20) should not only be a motivating factor but an attitude adjuster. Being a disciple of Christ brings new realizations and ways of living life.

But then, in order to live in God's kingdom it has to be that way. Not only is the call of Christ radical, living in the kingdom is (in today's language) extreme. There is nothing ordinary or natural about kingdom principles. Do any of us fully comprehend or practice such standards as:

- losing one's life in order to find it
- not amassing treasures on earth
- selling possessions and distributing to the poor
- turning the other cheek to an evildoer who would strike us
- really treating others as we want to be treated
- doing good to those who hate us
- giving our shirt to someone who took our coat
- loving our enemies and expecting nothing in return
- praying without meaningless repetition
- loving Christ more than family
- rejoicing when falsehoods have been spoken against believers

The list could go on. Considering such drastic statements, have any of us pledged full allegiance to the kingdom of God? And what would happen if we all lived this way? Obviously, there would be extraordinary changes in our personal lives and in the world if the followers of Christ *really* practiced the principles of the kingdom in a consistent manner.

Entrance into the kingdom of God requires repentance, meaning a change of mind. In that sense it is "radical," which etymologically means "to the root." It necessitates a thoroughgoing conversion or transformation to live according to God's standards. Because "radical" today can mean the left-wing militant, extremist, or free-thinking rebel, the word is used cautiously here and, hopefully, without exaggeration. Many Christians cringe at the idea of radical discipleship because of burdensome experiences with moral perfectionism or legalistic perversions of the faith. I'm not sure the term "radical" needs to be used as we nurture people, but during the growth process, there needs to be an increasing awareness that what we are called to is not ordinary. Bonhoeffer was clearly marked by the radical nature of these words from Jesus:

> *"Whoever desires to come after me, let him deny himself, and take up his cross, and follow me. For whoever desires to save his life will lose it, but whoever loses his life for my sake and the gospel's will save it. For what will it profit a man if he gains the whole world and loses his own soul? Or what will a man give in exchange for his soul? For whoever is ashamed of me and my words in this adulterous and sinful generation, of him the Son of Man also will be ashamed when He comes in the glory of His Father with the holy angels"* (Mark 8:34-38).

Christ's own disciples found His sayings to be difficult and not easy to comprehend, but He lovingly and patiently continued to walk and talk with them. The standards of the kingdom slowly sank in, and when they were put to the test after the acsension, the disciples exhibited a remarkable understanding of what Jesus had taught. Certainly, the idea of being a suffering servant had taken hold as they expended their lives for the sake of the gospel.

Embedded in the meaning of the "gospel" or *good news*, is the anticipated rule and reign of God. As the *good news* is proclaimed today in various forms, one could get the idea that it is the great tidings of peace and tranquility, happiness and prosperity, fulfillment and authenticity or even just hope of eternal life. The "good news" is that God has come into human history, established His kingdom and we can now know a new reality. Though not in fullness, the kingdom of God is in our midst, and we live accordingly, awaiting its ultimate triumph. The whole purpose of the world and the redemption story is the coming of the kingdom. The overarching call of Christ and to His kingdom must be acknowledged by the discipler and kept in the "corner of the eye" as the discipling process takes place.

In order to keep a proper perspective, the question, "What am I trying to produce?" should be asked from time to time. The call is not to a certain methodology or set of techniques that will make us attractive, successful Christians, but to a Person---one in whom we have complete trust. In practical terms, that means we obey His orders, follow His teaching, live a moral and ethical life, exercise humility in all circumstances, and are even willing to let go of those dear to us. Actually, this type of character *will* make us attractive, successful Christians, but it will be a by-product rather than a goal.

Excellent books have been written on what it means to be a follower of Christ. Personal holiness, sacrifice, spiritual disciplines, calling, mission, and a myriad of topics have been addressed by various authors, all contributing to an understanding of what it means to be a disciple of Christ. That is "discipleship" in its broad view, and as devoted adherents to His teachings, we will forever be pupils of His, continuous learners, as we pass from "one degree of glory to the next." (II Cor. 3:18)

Chapter II

HEEDING THE COMMISSION

The original 12 disciples spent approximately three years with Jesus, having accepted His summons to leave all and follow Him. When their personal disciplemaking process was concluding, Jesus commissioned these men with whom He had lived and worked to "go and make disciples" (Matt. 28:19). In so doing, He set forth a principle that has been an inspiration, challenge and perhaps a disappointment to many believers throughout the centuries.

First of all, an inspiration, because Jesus commanded it, and like all other Biblical commands, it is to be considered and obeyed. His commission puts within us a prompting, a motivation and direction for service within the kingdom of God. We are inspired because we know what we are to do. He stated it simply and directly. Perhaps even greater incentive comes from the fact that not only did Jesus command His followers to reproduce in making other disciples, He did it Himself. The disciplemaking mandate would have valid authorization just because the Son of God commanded it; however, extra impetus is attached because Jesus "earned His stripes" by giving Himself wholeheartedly to the task. In fact, it was Plan A.

There is a familiar anecdote that goes like this: When Jesus returned to heaven after the completion of His earthly ministry, an angel asked Him, "What plans do you have to continue the work you began on earth?" Jesus replied, "I left it in the hands of my disciples." The angel then asked, "What if they fail?" Jesus responded, "I have no other plan."

There is no question that the primary focus of Christ's energy during His public ministry was the training of His disciples. As Plan A, it was His priority. He gave Himself to the masses as well with their needs and questions, but His concentration was on the handful of men He selected. There is great inspiration in the fact that not only did Jesus establish a principle in the Great Commission, but by example He gave a plan for doing it. Selecting a small group of men with whom He could intensely work was His plan. He knew that disciples could not be mass-produced.

Secondly, the disciplemaking mandate is also a challenge because it is supracultural and has been obeyed in myriads of settings and circumstances throughout the centuries. Just how to carry out this plan has been a source of much thought and creativity for the followers of Christ. We know we are to do it, but how is the best way to go about the task? Believing that a providential God has "determined our appointed times and the boundaries of our habitation" (Acts 17:26), each Christian has had to face the challenge of reproducing disciples in a given location and time allotment on earth. From the apostles, to the church fathers, to the Reformers, to the present day, men and women have been discipled, and in each instance, it probably had unique features. Thankfully, no rigid method has been forced upon us, so the task will look differently in dissimilar cultures and at various points in time. The challenge in our contemporary American culture would involve the busyness, affluence and privitization which govern believers' lives, but certainly those who have gone before found their own set of challenges in their particular circumstances.

Thirdly, the Lord's plan has perhaps also been a disappointment to believers because it *is* Plan A. Getting up close and personal with a handful of people with the purpose of instructing them…*this* is what I am to do? Couldn't there be a more exciting, dramatic way of relaying the principles of the kingdom? Facing the reality of the Lord's plan has been cause for consternation. It just doesn't seem exhilarating enough. It's so behind the scenes, so thankless, so much time, so much patience, so much like child-raising.

The realization that Jesus was willing to do this is astounding, which is one of the many facets of the Incarnation that invokes wonder and awe. The God-man experiencing life on the earth He created, living among people and becoming "acquainted with grief," "oppressed and afflicted" (Is. 53) because of the human condition is cause for contemplation and reverence. With all the power accessible to Christ, His plan could have been quite different. He could have wowed the crowds with miracles, dynamic preaching and impressive displays of His might. He could have become well known quickly with His fame spreading far beyond the small geographic area to which He limited Himself. He could have "knocked people over" with talent, genius, and unbelievable capabilities. Instead, He came as a servant who simply walked and talked with a handful of men, allowing them to know Him in a personal way, instilling the truth in them by word and example. It's almost too undramatic and too ordinary considering who He was.

There have been times when I wished the commission of Christ were not so clear and direct. I would like to hold up to God my personality, gifts and talents and recommend they be a substitute for personal disciplemaking. After all, didn't He equip me with other abilities that I could spend all of my time developing? When I find so much satisfaction and fulfillment in another area, couldn't He "let me off the hook" and make an exception just for me? Because I am a person who enjoys a variety of creative expressions, life simply is not long enough to develop them fully in the way I would like. Couldn't I honor my Creator by concentrating on my musical skills, for instance, especially when I am told that it is a "real ministry" within the church and focus on the vast potential in arranging, conducting and performing great music? Do I really have to concern myself with teaching the younger women "what is good, to love their husbands, love their children, be sensible, workers at home, kind, and subject to their own husbands so the word of God may not be dishonored" (Titus 2:3-5), especially when it takes up valuable time that I could be investing in my music?

And what about my personality? By nature, I am very contented to be alone; in fact, I get worn out by people more quickly than others. And, in spite of my many years of working closely with women, I still score low on relational scales in personality tests! I could easily remind the Lord that I am not naturally equipped to get so involved with others.

Some have said that by example alone the qualities of the Titus II woman are caught and taught, so just by living a godly life I am "teaching" others what a disciple of Christ looks like. That would be easy enough. Others have said that if people really want to grow, they will observe the lives of the good examples around them and the Holy Spirit will do the rest. Without diminishing the importance of the godly example and the vital work of the Spirit, it is difficult to get around the model that Christ set forth. The "teaching-them-to-observe-all-that-I-commanded-you" part seems to involve more than an unconnected relationship with no accountability, especially considering the intensity of our present culture and its effect on people. The poignant II Tim. 2:2 principle of teaching what we have learned and entrusting that body of truth to faithful people who will in turn teach others, seems to involve much more than an impersonal example.

So, in a way there is a bit of a let-down as I realize that Jesus meant business with His plan. No matter what my gifts, reasons or excuses, I need to grasp the importance of what He did. If obedience to His command was not motivation enough, the sheer pragmatism of the results should be convincing. It works! There is no better way to grow people. Even though Christ's disciples were unsure of themselves at the time of His departure, within a short period of time they "turned the world upside down" (Acts 17:6). Illustrations abound in history as well as present times that the fruit of this type of reproduction is most substantial. There is no substitute for Christ's model of nurturing believers.

The challenge is in the doing. Because we are called to live out our humanity before our Creator and honor Him by enjoying the good gifts that have been given to us, we *can* develop the talents that have been entrusted into our care. The nobleman in Luke 19 severely chided the servant who buried what had been given to him, and we have trembled over the words, "from everyone who has been given much shall much be required" (Luke 12:48). God's grace has richly endowed His people with much, so that natural gifts are not to be ignored or left undeveloped. Many viable ministries with seemingly impressive results have been born out of gifted saints. Without diminishing their value, the commission of Christ to make disciples still exists as the premier effort of His people. Personal disciplemaking cannot be ignored, but instead held high and protected in practical ways involving energy and time. We each can only do so much. With this in mind, the challenge is to arrange other commitments, other "ministries," and other engagements around the high priority of "teaching others to observe" all that Christ commanded.

Chapter III

SCRIPTURAL PORTRAYAL

Throughout the general New Testament admonitions, the impression is given that teaching others by word and example is significant in establishing the principles needed for spiritual maturity. Whether it's in the church as a whole or for individual growth, the blend of spoken truth and modeled truth is an effective combination. Without doing a theological exegesis on the following passages, I merely want to offer them for consideration, with my own highlights and comments. They deserve more study and investigation than the treatment here.

1. THE EXAMPLE OF JESUS

Overriding all specific verses on this subject would be the example of Jesus and the approach He took to teaching doctrine and kingdom ideology. It was life-on-life, as indicated by the many phrases such as:

Matt. 5:1, 2: "…and after He sat down, His disciples came to Him. And opening His mouth He began to teach them…"

Matt. 12:1: "At that time Jesus went on the Sabbath through the grainfields, and His disciples became hungry and began to pick the heads of grain and eat."

Matt. 13:1, 2, 10: "…Jesus went out of the house and was sitting by the sea, and great multitudes gathered about Him, so that He got into a boat and sat down, and the whole multitude was standing on the beach…and the disciples came and said, 'Why so you speak to them in parables?'"

Matt. 14:15-21: In the feeding of the five thousand, the disciples were active in distributing the food to the multitude.

Mark 13:1: "As he was going out of the temple, one of His disciples said to Him, 'Teacher, behold what wonderful stones and what wonderful buildings!' And Jesus said to him…"

Luke 6:19, 20: "All the multitude were trying to touch Him, for power was from Him and healing them all. And turning His gaze on disciples, He began to say…"

Luke 8:1: "It came about soon afterwards that He began going about from one city and village to another proclaiming and preaching the kingdom of God; and the twelve were with Him."

Luke 9:1: "He called the twelve together and gave them power and authority over all the demons and to heal diseases. And He sent them out to proclaim the kingdom of God and to perform healing."

John 13:5: "He poured water into the basin and began to wash the disciples' feet and to wipe them with the towel with which He was girded."

John 18:1: "When Jesus had spoken these words, He went forth with His disciples over the ravine of the Kidron, where there was a garden, into which He Himself entered, and His disciples.

This is a sampling of scripture that indicates the "hands on" approach Jesus took in discipling. Repeated phrases such as, "and as they were traveling along," and "Jesus sat down and taught them, saying…" point to the balance the Twelve received in (1) verbal instruction, (2) watching Jesus handle different situations, and then (3) doing assignments themselves. The first four books of the New Testament contain this kind of activity.

2. THE GREAT COMMISSION

> Matt. 28:10, 20: "Go therefore and make disciples…*teaching them to observe* all that I commanded you…"

The word "observe" is intriguing because it connotes a different kind of knowing. *Tereo* in the Greek, it means to "pay attention to" or "keep what is learned and not lose it." *Knowing* something would mean to have the knowledge in one's head, acquainted with the facts and familiar with the content. *Observing* would involve "conforming one's action or practice to" (dictionary). In making disciples, part of the responsibility is to teach people that they are to pay close attention to the instruction of Christ and conform their actions to all that He commanded.

Just as the disciples were fortunate enough to hear Jesus teach and watch His attitudes and actions, resulting in their practice of the same, so they were to promote that kind of obedience in the disciples they would make.

3. OTHER NEW TESTAMENT ADMONITIONS

> I Cor. 4:16: "I exhort you therefore, be *imitators* of me."

> I Cor. 11:1: "Be *imitators* of me, just as I also am of Christ.

Paul was bold enough to come right out and say it. As a spiritual father to these people, he wanted them to follow in his steps and emulate his example. He offered himself as a model.

> Phil. 3:17: "…join in following my *example* and observe those who walk according to the *pattern* you have in us."

> Phil. 4:9: "The things you have *learned, received, heard* and *seen* in me, practice these things…"

Already in the early days of the church there were the counterfeits and those who proclaimed false doctrine. Jealous of the loyalty his converts would exhibit to his teaching, Paul reminds the Philippians of all they had not only heard, but seen in his life. The example of his life gave credibility to the genuine nature of the truth taught.

> I Thess. 1:5-7: "…just as you know what kind of men we proved to be among you for your sake. You also *became imitators* of us and the Lord…so that you *became an example* to all the believers."

> I Thess. 2:5-12: "…but we proved to be gentle among you…having a fond affection for you…we were well-pleased to impart to you not only the gospel of God, but *our own lives,*…we were *exhorting, encouraging,* and *imploring* each of you as a father would his own children.

These two chapters in I Thessalonians are favorites of mine because of the deep affection and feeling conveyed by Paul for these people with whom he and the other apostolic team members had lived. He likens their ministry among these people to a nursing mother tenderly caring for her children. They worked day and night so as not to be a financial burden to the Thessalonians and endured hardship in their midst. The people were dear to Paul. He developed a "fond affection" for them, and the team behaved uprightly and blamelessly in their presence. Not only did they convey the gospel in power, full conviction and in the Holy Spirit, but they proved what kind of men they were day by day. What a potent combination! Paul commends the people for their own work of faith and steadfast labor. They had indeed followed the example of the team and in turn became examples to all the believers in Achaia and Macedonia.

II Tim. 2:2: "The things which you have heard from me in the presence of many witnesses, these entrust to faithful men, who will be *able to teach others* also."

Perhaps the most often-used verse in the matter of disciplemaking, II Tim. 2:2 conveys the reproductive cycle necessary for the success of the same. In fact, disciplemaking isn't complete until it has come full circle. The turn-around effect in this verse is four generations. Paul had been taught, and then he taught Timothy, who now will teach others in order that they may teach others. I especially like the phrase, "in the presence of many witnesses," which indicates that this was no private doctrine or interpretation that Paul passed on to Timothy, but was observed by others to be the truth. Paul recognized the need for accountability and made himself liable to the scrutiny of many. What he proclaimed could be trusted.

Titus 2:3-5: "Older-women are to...*teach what is good*, so that they may *encourage the young women*...so that the word of God will not be dishonored."

These verses are specifically geared towards women, of course, and give concrete areas that the older/younger woman relationship is to address. Each of these traits in this passage can be taught and modeled, and should be, if they are to be learned effectively. It is of great interest that in the Cretan culture where Paul describes them as "liars, evil beasts and lazy gluttons" (Tit. 1:12), the operative plan was for the older women to teach the younger women the virtues listed (2:3-5). For a disintegrated society, the plan was grass-roots, life-on-life, personal and loving. It seems so straightforward and plain, so fundamental and uncomplicated, yet so right. The development of this type of character would renew the culture and stop the decline. It would be "here a little and there a little," with the education being thorough and practical. I've been grateful for this passage of scripture because it gives such clear direction for women.

Other scripture could be used to support the concept of word and example in disciplemaking but the above are fairly clear and easy to understand. The example of Jesus is overwhelmingly persuasive, and then the directives by Paul affirm the same.

CHAPTER IV

DEFINING THE TERM

Having established the broader scope of discipleship as a follower of Christ learning the ways of the kingdom and living under the reign of our Lord, the term should be defined in a more narrow sense. "Discipleship" means different things to different people. From time to time, it has become a buzzword in the evangelical world when a new method is promoted or there is a renewed interest in disciplemaking. Many evangelicals view it as a program within the church…a class that is taught for so many weeks. ("Oh, yes, I took a discipleship course once.")

Many Christians view discipleship as something that new believers need to go through for a while. Some view it as more of a one-on-one mentoring relationship. Some view any edifying relationship as discipleship. ("We're discipling each other.") "Discipleship" seems to have many definitions, especially to those who are not actively involved in it. The more one is engaged in the dynamics of disciplemaking, the clearer the definition becomes. I've had to restrain myself in conversation when someone refers to a casual association with someone as "discipleship." The temptation is to say, "No, no, no. It means so much more than that."

No matter how far along each of us is in our understanding of discipleship, we probably all agree that it is a life-long process of gaining clarity on what it means to be a follower of Christ. There needs to be (1) a growing comprehension of who He is, (2) a growing articulation of what He taught and (3) a growing ability to flesh-out what He taught in daily life. As we gain knowledge, we should also increase in our ability to verbalize what we know. In my experience, the emphasis on the first has been fairly constant with all the seminars, workshops, Bible studies and courses available to Christians. But these have not necessarily produced a capability to articulate clearly what one is learning. Many times I have heard Christians say things like, "Wow, that was a fantastic message. I can't really tell you what he said, but the speaker was great." Or, "My friend keeps asking me all these theological questions. I need to give her my pastor's phone number." Surely, in careful disciplemaking, there should be an emphasis on becoming one who can teach others. Learning to articulate one's beliefs, knowing that answers can be found to tough questions, and having the confidence to relay truth is essential to being a disciple of Christ.

Years ago, a good friend frequently asked me, "What have you been learning lately?" Not to quiz me or put me on the spot, she was genuinely interested in how I was growing. Every time I saw Sharon, I knew there was the possibility of this question, so I learned to formulate my thoughts in order to give her an answer. It might have been regarding a book I was reading, some Scriptural passage, a cassette I had listened to, or a very practical area in raising my young children. Her simple question made me evaluate and articulate what had been going on in my life.

If a growing comprehension of the faith is not occurring, nor is there a developing ability to articulate what is learned, I would say that true discipleship is not happening. We certainly need to help Christians get beyond the notion that the pastor and other "fulltime" staff members do all the teaching and answer all the questions. Our minds would be much more engaged if we saw our individual responsibilities here. A proper understanding of the priesthood of the believer would also be helpful…that we are all priests before God, not just the professional clergy.

"Disciple" from the Greek, *mathetes,* means "learner" or "pupil." But the word carries with it the idea that the learning is "by use and practice." So this is more than just a head knowledge, but a learning that comes from exercise as well. A disciple, in the true sense of the word is one who is learning by thinking and doing.

Recognizing the continual nature of this learning and doing, a true disciple is one in process all of his life. Beginning with the infancy stage, a "babe in Christ" who desires to learn and obey the teachings of Christ, is just as much a disciple as one who has walked with the Lord 40 years. Characteristics of mature believers are acquired through continual flux, modifications, realizations and exposure to deeper truths. Profound changes are made along the way. There is no predictable sequence or stipulated pace in the acquisition of mature attributes. We are lifelong learners. And since we will retain our humanity in the life to come, we will be learners for eternity as well. It's an invigorating thought that there will always be something to discover, to find out, and yet another area in which to gain knowledge.

Jesus used the dynamics of a small group for this learning to take place. Seeing and doing is often more easily caught when there are others to observe. As the premier model of discipleship then, there was:

- ✧ the acquiring of content
- ✧ the example of Christ Himself
- ✧ the doing of special tasks assigned by Christ.

Based on these observations, I have constructed a simple definition of discipleship, including the basic components necessary to execute the commission given to each one of us.

> *Learning and applying the principles of the Bible within the context of a committed relationship with another or others with the goal of reproducing what is learned.*

Learning – Because "disciple" means "learner," this is necessary first and foremost. Knowledge is key in order to learn, so there has to be content. Jesus *taught* His disciples. "Learn-*ing*" would also imply that it is ongoing.

Applying – It is more than filling a notebook with outlines and facts. Acquiring knowledge is the first step in order that there can also be an acquiring of new habits and practices as well. Knowing correct doctrine can be life-changing. Good doctrine has many practical applications. The behavior (attitudes and actions) of a disciple is bound to change if the knowledge is applied.

Principles – These are the unchanging truths of scripture that are supra-cultural and apply to any period of time and to any ethnicity. They are the precepts that must be learned if one is to be truly Christian. They are the tenets and beliefs upon which our convictions are based.

Bible – Our textbook and authority, the Bible provides the anchor for discipling. Although subjects beyond the pages of scripture are discussed, the conclusions should not contradict the truths taught in scripture.

Context – There is an arena, a setting, in which the dynamics of growth take place. It provides safety for the disciple because it isn't "Lone Ranger" learning. The environment is both a protection and an encouragement.

Committed – This connotes obligation and loyalty, not, "I'll come, if it's convenient." There is dedication to both the long-term process and the actual meeting times.

Relationship – Jesus connected with His disciples and they were in an alliance with Him and with each other. There was a mutual understanding of the process and they profited from each other's questions and responses.

Another/Others – Disciplemaking involves two people at the least… the discipler and the disciple. Advantages and disadvantages of one-on-one will be discussed later, but suffice it to say that a relationship is *always* present when discipling is occurring. If more than two, it cannot be a large group, obviously, or the relationship between the discipler and those in the group will be impersonal.

Goal – Discipleship is not an end in itself; it is a means to an end. Jesus had a bigger picture in mind when He developed an intimate relationship with His disciples. There was a long-term objective.

Reproducing – Duplicating the growth process should be the healthy cycle of discipleship. Grateful for the maturity and awareness gained through being discipled, the disciple now passes on the truth so that others can experience the same kind of growth.

This is a basic, bottom-line definition that is easy to convey to those considering a discipleship group. I've expanded the statement many times to include other elements present in such a group, but where to stop in describing the process is always the challenge. Obviously, much more happens than just discussing principles of scripture; however, discussing principles of scripture is indispensable to the definition. As seen in the curriculum, the subjects are varied with emphasis on the culture and family as well as on doctrine, so this basic definition merely provides a foundation for the purpose of the group.

Just a word about the difference between discipling and mentoring. In brainstorming sessions with other women, we have split hairs in trying to decipher the difference. Certainly there is an overlap at times, and putting a label on what is occurring might be fruitless. There is mentoring in discipling and there is discipling in mentoring. The difference seems to be in the arrangement and purpose of the relationship between two people. When there is an agreed-upon structure, say, of two-hour weekly meetings for one year with the purpose of learning and applying Biblical truths in a committed accountable relationship, the arrangement seems to be more "formalized." Using the model of Jesus and His disciples, this would come close to that description. Mentoring is more often born out of specific need or enjoyment and can be quite unstructured. The get-together or phone conversation can occur whenever the need arises, and can involve any variety of subjects, from cooking to raising children. I have a quilting mentor who has always made herself available to me. At a moment's notice, I can run over for her input on my project, and I respect her advice and years of experience very much.

An older acquaintance of mine who has worked with women for years in leading Bible studies, speaking at conferences and teaching missionaries around the world put it this way: "I tell the women in my church that I'm available any time they want to call and get together. But don't ask to meet with me regularly, as I can't commit to discipling at this point in my life." She refers to herself as a mentor of women these days because of health limitations with both her husband and herself.

It is a good exercise to write a definition of discipleship. Not only does it clarify the necessary features of such an activity for the leader of the group, but it will help in setting the goals for the allotted time of study together.

CHAPTER V

INTERNAL MOTIVATION

Motivation for engaging in disciplemaking can come from several directions. Ideally, the fact that Jesus did it and commanded it should be motivation enough. In the company of other believers, mentioning that the concept of discipleship is biblical, or that it's a command, makes little impact because it represents the all-too-familiar Christian vocabulary. The objective of this chapter is to expand on motivational factors found within the body of Christ itself. This is the internal evidence for the need to make disciples.

After all, the bigger picture *is* the church. God instituted the church as His plan for this age, and history reveals the effectiveness of the church when it has been strong, and conversely, its lack of impact when it has been weak. The church is the place of belonging for the believer. Automatically placed within the universal church of Jesus Christ at the time of conversion, that membership is expressed in a local body of believers. The local church is the place where we are connected with other believers, where we participate in the sacraments, where we discover and use our gifts, where we edify and enlighten each other, where we comfort and encourage, laugh and weep with each other. This is where the equipping takes place so that the work can be carried on and perpetuated through the years.

Individual local churches have devised many plans for spiritual and numerical growth. There can be numerous programs that will engage people in a variety of activities to help them feel connected and a part of that church. There have been a multitude of books, seminars and conferences that generate ideas for developing the various ministries of the church. Keeping people involved and active seems to be a high priority as well as being able to offer many programs to those without who might be seeking church affiliation.

Programs can give a false sense of success in a church just by the sheer numbers of active people participating. This has contributed to the pseudo strength that characterizes the evangelical church in America today. Having a busy church life does not necessarily contribute to the spiritual depth of that body. It has been observed that Christianity in America is 3,000 miles wide and an inch thick. Having had 40 years of employment within the local church, Tom and I know for certain that activity does not necessarily produce substance in the believer's life. It does not guarantee maturity nor assure that one is thinking Christianly. For years we have asked the question, "Why does the church have so little cultural impact?" It is our perception that the church herself has become culturalized to the point that there is little difference between those within the church and without. So there is definitely internal motivation for engaging in life-on-life training. There is no substitute for personal disciplemaking. Listed are a few reasons within the church for doing what Christ commanded us to do.

1. BABIES REQUIRE CARE

In the evangelical world, it is quite common to get excited about someone's spiritual new birth and never give thought to the nurturing process. If a woman gave birth to a baby and left the infant to fend for itself, we would be horrified and accuse the woman of inhumane treatment and child abuse. That type of concern is not often expressed when a "babe in Christ" is in our midst. Who is going to feed this new baby? What will be the diet of this new creation in Christ? Who is going to pat this new baby on the back, cuddle, comfort and encourage? Who will be the examples that demonstrate how to walk, how to stand up again when the stumbling happens and how to develop skills that will aid in proper development?

Throughout the years, Tom and I have observed that new believers grow best when they are born into a built-in care system, such as a small group. They immediately have a "family" that will provide the protection, care and encouragement needed for their growth. We have concluded that "group evangelism" is really the best method for bringing people to faith. Repeatedly, we have seen small group Bible study members invite non-believing friends into the circle and, over time, these friends are literally "loved to Christ." The relational dynamics, the fun of community life, the truth that is studied, and the genuine sharing of each other's lives is quite irresistible. Authenticity is highly appealing and difficult to oppose. Babies grow best when they are in healthy families.

Many, however, aren't born into that environment and even feel abandoned. The seed of faith was planted, but little nurturing has occurred. Many believers remain in infancy even though they professed Christ several years back. Maybe they are participating in the "goodies" of the church and "playing on the playground" with other children, but no one has taken an interest in their personal diet, care, and development. Healthy foundations have not been established for a life with substance and direction. The church needs to seriously look at its new believers and those who remain in spiritual infancy.

2. Examples Are Needed

People within the church are products of the culture, and bear the marks of powerful influences that dictate their lives. New models are needed to demonstrate new ways of thinking and living.

In spite of the heavy emphasis of the last 35 years on individualism ("I Gotta Be Me," "I need to be my own person," "I'm free to be me," "I Did It My Way"), people still yearn for good examples on how to do life. All of us are encouraged, inspired, motivated and challenged by people who model specific virtues and characteristics that are needed in our own lives. Certainly a chapter like Hebrews 11 was given for our encouragement. I've been thankful for these models of faith who endured all kinds of circumstances in their real life existence on earth, looking ahead and never grasping what they longed to see. Not unflawed, God still chose to use them as examples for our benefit.

I'll never forget a survey taken in our local high school in the Chicago area in the mid-70's. The question asked of the students (and then reported in the newspaper) was, "Who do you admire the most?" The vast majority responded, "No one." Demonstrating the growing individualism of the time, the paper also quoted an eighth-grade student about her future goals: "I think you just have to be yourself. You don't have to be guided by what people have done in the past or what older people are doing now." Even if it was a trendy answer, it represented the emphasis of the culture at that time...as well as the reason why, after 30 years, we presently live with an ultra-individualism that is embedded in the psyche of people.

Because the church has to undo what the culture has done to individuals, it needs to provide flesh-and-blood examples of the godly traits needed to redo individuals. God, in His kindness to women, has given specific guidelines and patterns to follow. Certainly the Proverbs 31 woman is everything most women would want to be, and the Titus 2 passage gives particulars that elevate womanhood to a high and honorable position. This knowledge from scripture is reinforced when it is modeled by godly women in the church. Biblical virtues now stand in such contrast to the present culture that we can no longer assume that women know what these virtues mean, especially if they have had no role models. In the discipling process, the relational intimacy provides this needed element in an up-close-and-personal way. Perhaps this is how the success of the church should be measured, instead of by the number of programs or members. The local church should be a resource center of believers who can teach the truth by word and modeled behavior. Edgar A. Guest captured this idea in his often-quoted poem:

> *"I had rather see a sermon than to hear one any day.*
> *I had rather one should walk with me than merely*
> *show the way.*
> *The eye's a better pupil and more willing than the ear;*
> *Fine council is confusing but examples always clear.*
> *And the best of all the preachers are those who*
> *live their creeds;*
> *For to see the good in action is what everybody needs.*
> *I can soon learn how to do it if you'll let me see it done;*
> *I can watch your hands in action, but your tongue too*
> *fast may run.*
> *And the lectures you deliver may be very wise and true,*
> *But I'd rather get my lesson by observing what you do.*
> *For I may misunderstand you and the high advice*
> *you give,*
> *But there's no misunderstanding how you act and*
> *how you live."*

3. Christians Need to Disciple For Their Own Health

Many Christians are in poor health today. They are "eating" too much and not exercising enough. They sit and soak and take in one big meal after another. The vast smorgasbord of CD's, conferences, seminars, Bible studies, films, retreats, messages and workshops provides the opportunity to ingest all kinds of information, and it's all "exciting." To be current with other evangelicals, many believers read "in vogue" books and align themselves with certain speakers or Bible studies to be in step with other believers doing the same.

A certain kind of spirituality is attached to all this and it provides the feeling that "walking with the Lord" involves this kind of participation. Yet it seems that few Christians develop their minds, learning to think beyond the comfortable Christian vocabulary that permeates the church. And even fewer can intelligently discuss their faith and defend it.

To be healthy, the calories need to get burned up. A different attitude needs to become the norm in the church, such as, "I take in that I may give out." Or, "I take in because I'm giving it out." A sponge is a good example of this action. It gets dipped in water then squeezed, in order to be useful. The information that fills my life needs to be squeezed out so that I may have a healthy balance between the two. There is great joy in studying *on behalf* of others. Going to the bookshelf, pulling out some resources and studying a subject because someone brought it up and needs an answer, is very satisfying. Preparing material for an informal coffee where a particular issue will be discussed is quite rewarding. We find ourselves thinking, searching the scriptures, praying, and checking out good literature because we want to encourage the life of the mind as well as the heart. We're highly motivated because people we love are genuinely inquisitive, questioning or puzzled by something.

Could this be, in part, what the Lord was referring to when He said, "When you lose your life, you find it" (Matt. 10:39)? Instead of reading the Bible just for me, spending time in prayer just for me, listening to taped lectures just for me, I find myself engaging in those activities because I need to have something to give. And although I'm doing it for the sake of others, I profit the most. In giving up my own time in order to do these things, I develop, grow and become the person God really wants me to be. In expending mental and physical energy for the sake of others, I learn that in giving, there truly is receiving. And the receiving is abundant.

What a different dynamic we would have in the evangelical community if the majority of believers were occupied with nurturing growth in others! Our conversations would be rich as we consulted each other for ideas, materials, and means of instructing and encouraging people. We would be probing each other's minds on cultural challenges and ways of influence. There is no doubt that our health would improve. There would be strength and energy available we presently do not experience.

4. Church Leadership Needs Fellow Workers

If the pastoral staff truly believes their task is "the equipping of the saints, for the work of the ministry, to the building up of the body of Christ" (Eph. 4:12), then they should take the lead in this matter of discipleship. Because the leadership team sets the standard for the church, there would be an acceptance throughout the body of this emphasis and responsibility. When there is a growing number of men who have personally been discipled by the pastors in the church and are now doing the same, the ministry becomes more broad-based. The ongoing care and counsel in church life should be the responsibility of more that just the paid staff.

Likewise, women in leadership should be actively equipping other women to do the same. This would develop an "others-mentality" of intentionally becoming acquainted with new women in the church, "keeping an eye out" for those who need someone to come alongside, and recognizing those who are teachable and available. Nothing is more satisfying than to see women develop in their abilities to teach and care for other women. Most women have instinctive "shepherd" qualities, and they just have to grow in their knowledge of what they believe and how to communicate that in order to be trusted servants in the church. Personally, it is a delight to be surrounded by so many capable women who are good teachers and role models. My life is rich as well as challenging because these women make me think.

The "iron-sharpening-iron" principle is always at work when we are together.

The church leadership team cannot really expect disciplemaking to occur within the body unless the team itself is engaged in the process themselves. Resistance would come from the time factor or limiting oneself to a small number of people for an extended period of time. In our church, each pastor spends two years with one discipleship group of four to seven men. These are weekly meetings of approximately two hours in length with breaks for the summer, holidays, etc. The women's groups vary from one to two years. Also weekly meetings, they vary from two to three hours in length with summer and holiday breaks as well. Probably without exception, those leading such groups would say it is the most rewarding time investment they could make. There is great satisfaction in working with a small band of teachable people. The dividends in close relationships are great as well as the multiplication factor. However, if the leadership team is threatened by the development of capable people within the church, want to maintain a safe distance between pastor and parishioner, or if they have a controlling, dictatorial attitude toward ministry, this kind of disciplemaking will not take place. One needs to delight in the expansion of gifts and abilities in others rather than be intimidated by them.

So the condition of the church itself is a motivating factor in making disciples. Other reasons could be listed, but these are primary in the ongoing work of a local body. This is not to say that other methods of working with people are ineffective, but to underscore the plan that the Master Teacher had in establishing the church. He taught His small band of disciples so they could "do the work of the ministry" and build His church.

Chapter VI

EXTERNAL MOTIVATION

Francis Schaeffer was saying in the 1960's that we were living in post-Christian times. Many found that term difficult to accept in those days, but as the "dominoes began to fall," as he predicted, it became clear that he was right. For those immersed in church work and the Christian sub-culture, as Tom and I were, life continued pretty much the same with a few adjustments. We had not been trained to engage culture or even study it. Christians were told to separate from "the world" and get involved in "the work of the Lord."

That all changed for Tom and me as our lives filled with young adults who were products of the culture. They were at our dinner table and in our living room, examples of existential philosophy and the growing relativism of the time. For me, a wake-up call came one evening as our Thursday night group gathered in our living room for our weekly study of the book of Romans. About 16 in the group, it was comprised of singles, ages 20-30, most of whom smoked cigarettes (during the study), most were marijuana users, some of the guys were just back from Viet Nam, and probably the majority were sexually active. Enthusiastic about the study each week, they came expectantly, eager for the dialogue that would occur. As the absolute truth of the scripture began to sink in, it clashed with the relativistic mindsets that most of them had, so our discussions were rigorous, animated and stimulating. (Those were the days when truth was still sought.)

One of the pretty young women in the group, Tasha, spoke up, and her casually expressed words impacted me like a bolt of lightning. She said, "I've always considered myself to be a good person. But now I'm realizing that what *I* think is good and what *God* thinks is good are two different things. I guess I need to learn to think like God thinks, but that's really hard." She considered herself "good," yet I knew she smoked marijuana, did cocaine on weekends, and prided herself in carefully selecting her sexual partners. But with all sincerity, she considered herself to be "good." When I was growing up, "good" was clearly defined by the church *and* society, and there's no way she would have fit that label. She would have been a bad girl.

The reality of the post-Christian culture impacted me with force and I could hardly open my mind to what lay ahead, it was so frightening. Words had lost their meaning and were being redefined. The standards of the Bible were no longer a yardstick by which to measure behavior. The autonomous self was now the essence of all things. As Tom and I were discussing the evening after everyone had left, I remember saying, "Boy, we have got our work cut out for us!" And that's been true for anyone who has grasped the secular nature of our culture, its effects on people and the disintegration of the traditions and standards we've always held dear. (By the way, many in that Thursday evening group came to faith in Christ, and as their minds became more and more Christian, lifestyles changed dramatically. Learning to "think like God thinks" produced a whole new way of living.)

Our culture is much farther down the road now than what is depicted in the above 1970's illustration. Our concern is not so much to Christianize our society as it is to save our civilization. The emphasis on absolute freedom without restraint has given complete reign to the human appetite in any area. Post-modernity has discredited traditional forms of authority and age-old standards of beauty and behavior. It ignores the abiding virtues that have governed human affairs, and has created intellectual chaos for anyone trying to establish operative norms.

Can all this be turned around? It would be nice to have a repeat of the First Great Awakening (1730s-1740s) with another George Whitefield and Jonathan Edwards stepping up to the plate. This would give Christians a shortcut to all the hard work that has to be done in clearing away the rubble in people's lives and re-laying foundations. Or perhaps things are so bad that the pendulum will swing back by itself. Knowing that God in His providence directs spiritual awakenings, and not knowing if we've gone as far as we can go, it behooves the Christian to think critically and teach others to do the same. Truth must be taught in arenas of accountability because, unfortunately, Christians themselves are so culturalized, their discerning capabilities are weak. Also, unfortunately, the collective Christian mind has seriously atrophied in recent decades to the point that critical participation in the culture is severely limited, because believers haven't developed a worldview that enables them to assess the milieu around them.

So the condition of our civilization demands more than comfortable Bible studies that maintain the status quo of believers. If we truly view ourselves as "salt" and "light," we must see our responsibility in practicing Godly virtues in the public square as well as in the church and home. Because of the tenacious nature of the culture, believers need accountability, committed prayer partners and comrades who are also engaged in the battle at hand. The discipler needs to make certain that those in the group are clear on a number of critical areas.

1. Creation Mandates

When developing our theology, origin is of extreme importance. The first two chapters of Genesis are key in our position on human identity, sexuality, the relationship of men and women, marriage, family and work. Since all of these were established before the fall, they were ordained by God for the entire human race. It is from the creation account that we build our premise on these all-important matters that are under attack today. One who identifies himself as a Christian must be able to address these creation mandates that have provided the foundation for every civilization on earth.

2. Doctrinal Stability

In order to think clearly and correctly in the midst of religious disarray and its many forms of spiritual experiences, one has to have feet firmly planted in sound doctrine. The 10 major areas of theology should be known by believers, with a growing comprehension of each area every time the material is covered. The areas are:

- Bibliology – the Bible
- Theology Proper – God the Father
- Christology – God the Son
- Pneumatology – the Holy Spirit
- Angelology - Angels
- Anthropology - Man
- Hamartiology - Sin
- Soteriology - Salvation
- Ecclesiology – the Church
- Eschatology – Last Things

Seeing professing Christians getting caught up in cults and other misrepresentations of the faith is heartbreaking, yet predictable, if they don't know what they believe.

3. Mind Development

There are reasons why this age has been referred to as the "age of non-reason." When newspapers and periodicals admit they are written at a fifth grade level, and the sound-byte explanation of issues is the norm, most minds are not exercised to think beyond the surface, formulate categories in which to assess the matters of concern and reason one's convictions. We need to be humble enough to admit that this generation has given up on the life of the mind and all of us have been affected. There needs to be a commitment to the process of mind development. After all, one can gather information quickly (especially in this technological age), but one does not always understand quickly. Reading at a higher level and perhaps writing down what is read (as writing always takes thoughts out of the abstract and makes them part of the thinking mechanism), viewing books as part of the human condition and not just tools for a particular subject (such as in school), and having time for contemplation should be encouraged in believers today. Reading history and authors who take people beyond themselves is so important. Perhaps an understanding of the structure and purpose of classical learning could be developed.

"What have you been reading lately?" should be a typical question Christians ask each other (and it would generate a fine conversation around the dinner table). Tom meets twice a month for lunch with a small group of men who are reading G.K. Chesterton together. The discussions are stimulating, as well as encouraging to men who perhaps didn't think they would be interested in that kind of literature. There are women's groups as well that meet regularly to report on the books they have been reading.

In response then to today's culture, the discipling process should promote mind development. Our minds are gifts from God that need to be exercised and expanded to be effectively useful. He has also equipped many throughout history with great minds that have contributed a wealth of literature which can stimulate our thinking and give us endless pleasure.

4. Secular Deterrent

The effects of the modern world are powerful. Modernity speaks of all the technology, commercialism, amusements, consumerism, globalism, lifestyles and attitudes that go together to define our modern world. Being secularized means there is a preoccupation with all this…the here and the now…with a diminished view of eternal values. What is currently happening is one's main focus and pursuit.

Due to the prevailing power of modernity, when the day-to-day routine is basically work and providing for one's self or family, a person is quite vulnerable to being secularized. Life has to be more than work. Today, a person will insert amusements into life purposefully as a reprieve from continuous work. Many think they owe it to themselves to play golf, watch TV, attend movies and ballgames *because* they work arduous hours. Leisure is now seen as amusement…a diversion from the work routine.

Historically, the word "leisure" connoted the betterment of the person for the betterment of culture, which involved a cessation of work in order that one could read, contemplate, and improve as a person. Thus, society itself would be improved if its individual members had leisure time. Since few people today understand leisure in this way, the "rat race" is on, and life is primarily work, with amusements added for diversion. There is no means in a person's life to prevent secularization. The here-and-the-now is of utmost importance.

Times of spiritual awakening or renewal have helped societies in regaining an eternal perspective and a view beyond the present.

But these times (which have lasted from several weeks to several years) are difficult to sustain if there is not a grassroots effort to perpetuate dynamic godliness. If revival brings a person back to life and reawakens a relationship with Christ, then the church should be ready to provide the nutritional regimen needed to sustain that vitality.

Meeting with a discipleship group is a safety implement that guards against the pressures of secularism. For the person involved, it provides an impetus to develop a Christian mind and other spiritual disciplines as well as a safety net, should circumstances in life change suddenly. There have been women in my groups, who without warning, were plunged into tragedy so intense, it dramatically altered their lives. Having a trusted group with whom to weep, pray, and continue to study, protected them against bitterness and paralyzing sorrow. Their minds continued to be filled with the truth, and there was a loving accountability that kept them on track when temptations to "stuff it" were intense.

It doesn't have to be tragedy that proves the need for such a group. The strain of a secular culture is not only wearisome, but numbing. The "frog in the pot" illustration, where the frog adapts to the rising water temperature, unaware that he is boiling to death, is a vivid portrayal of what is presently happening to many of us. No one is exempt from this possibility. "Take heed to him who stands lest he fall" (I Cor. 10:12).

For the discipler, especially, there is strong motivation to remain diligent because of the additional challenge of being a teacher and example. James 3:1 issues a warning indicating that teachers assume greater responsibility: "Let not many of you become teachers, my brethren, knowing that as such we shall incur a stricter judgment."

On the positive side, the preparation for a weekly group is beneficial in deterring the pressures of culture because the mind and heart are engaged together in such a healthy and profitable endeavor. Praying for those in the group, preparing material for the upcoming session, and evaluating the progress is a wonderful responsibility that both protects the discipler as well as fortifies him. Life is then more than just work and amusements. There is a built-in mechanism to direct mental and physical energies elsewhere. There is a stimulus for learning and a safeguard against the power of a secular culture.

Chapter VII

EQUIPPING THE EQUIPPERS

A discipler is one who equips others. He supplies the provisions to those in his care so they will be adequately outfitted to carry on. The dictionary definition of "equip" is: "to furnish for service or action by appropriate provisioning." The equipper is the primary human agent through which God chooses to bring others to maturity.

A crucial passage in understanding our life within the body of Christ is the fourth chapter of Ephesians. The main offices God designated for the church are that of apostle, prophet, evangelist and pastor/teacher. Some list these as the "teaching gifts," or "up-front gifts," but they are indeed gifts that God has furnished the church with in order that the saints can "attain the unity of the faith" (4:13) and reach maturity. As these gifts are exercised, or to put it another way, as these offices are executed, the body of Christ will be built up and edified. Obviously, this would pertain especially to those who care for the body as shepherds and teachers…those who are concerned with substance in the lives of believers. They look for ways to nurture growth and to aid in the sanctification process. God gave instructors and trainers "for the *equipping* of the saints, for the work of service, to the building up of the body of Christ…" (4:11). If the saints are equipped, then the equippers have done their work. What would be the basic qualifications of one who equips? What does an equipper look like? And how do you know when a person has been equipped?

Tom and I were returning from a retreat where leadership development was the topic of the weekend and we asked ourselves those questions. While he drove, I wrote down seven areas of qualifications we believed were necessary in the life of one who is interested in equipping others. These are basic elements that should be present, not in full maturity necessarily, but enough so that proper equipping can take place. They, at least, provide a goal toward which to work…either to reach for one's self or to achieve in the lives of others.

1. Assurance of salvation

An equipper should be secure in Christ. Being familiar with Biblical content that speaks to assurance of salvation, our position in Christ, God's unconditional forgiveness, the ongoing high priestly work of Christ on our behalf and our acceptance before the Father should be included here. (Scripture for this will be listed in the curriculum.)

An equipper should be able to articulate his own testimony to the point of leading another to salvation. Having thought through one's own journey to faith is vital in being able to give intelligent replies for those who ask the reason "for the hope that is within" (I Pet. 3:15). Thinking through one's own testimony enables the equipper to recognize the signposts and essential elements of his own unique story. Every person has a story, and no two are alike.

2. Comprehension of the Christian faith

An equipper should have a personal knowledge of the Bible, know the categories and order of the books and be a self-feeder in personal study. Not always relying on extra-biblical material for inspiration or self-help, he should be able to have satisfying study on his own, using the Bible as his text.

Three areas that are necessary in having a comprehension of the Christian faith:

◆ Doctrine

The basic tenets of our faith should be known, such as the cardinal doctrines of Christianity:

- the Existence of God
- the Authority of the Scriptures
- the Virgin Birth
- the Deity of Christ
- the Blood Atonement
- Justification by Faith
- Final Judgment

There needs to be an understanding of the essential truths that are foundational to our faith. Acquiring apologetic skills as well to defend the tenets of Christianity should be a goal and a lifelong aspiration. Developing convictions in doctrine will keep a person grounded and able to discern what is right and wrong with all the religious language and practice around him.

◆ History

There needs to be a growing understanding of the journey of the church, from the New Testament times to the present. It is vital to know some of the significant historical dates, events, documents and writings that remain important and enrich the life of today's church. A general knowledge, not necessarily comprehensive, is most helpful in identifying turning points and critical periods in church history. It gives a better perspective on the present, helps protect against repeating errors and provides a mainstream of doctrine in which to fit. Besides, it is so interesting as well as enlightening!

Tom and I have seen many "ah-ha's" expressed by people once the pieces of the historical puzzle are put in place.

♦ Worldview

The grid through which we look at life is developed from a growing knowledge of doctrine and history. It is said that everyone has a philosophy of life, but usually not identified. An equipper should at least be putting that grid in place and able to identify how he approaches life. How does he evaluate life? How does he "do" life? What is the lens through which he looks at life? Developing a Christian mind would be part of this process, of course. Being able to think Christianly about all of life is part of this growth.

Toward the end of our time together, I ask the women in my group to define their worldview, write it out and read it to the others. It usually is quite a mental exercise to reduce the basic elements of a life philosophy to a definition where it can be stated succinctly. Certainly, part of equipping people is helping them define their worldview…at least to think it through. It matters in every area of life.

3. Home life

Biblical principles should work at home, otherwise, whatever a person says is weakened. If married, the husband/wife relationship should be following God's design for marriage. Children ought to be generally characterized by respect and obedience. Homes do not need to be perfect (or none of us would qualify), but they should support the ministry we do and not contradict it. Most seasoned workers in the church would admit that when things are not right at home, there is a lack of confidence or enthusiasm to do what we are called to do. Having a home life characterized by delight in each other, enjoyment in child-raising and the various stages of life, harmony, and order gives tremendous impetus and freedom to the one called to teach others. Troubles at home can sap a person of mental, emotional, physical and spiritual energy. Rather than be freed up to give, the person is bound by concerns that restrain. Even the most gifted, energetic worker will eventually wear down and lose heart if the home life continues to be an anxiety.

4. Hospitality

Because nurturing growth in others involves more than factual information and material, hospitality is central to a life-on-life participation with others. One of the prerequisites for eldership in I Tim. 3, for example, is that a man's home be known for its hospitality. It is my opinion that personal care and attention is best demonstrated in the home. No matter how lovely the church building, or another facility, being in someone's home provides the opportunity for a different kind of intimacy. The home is a place of service. Sharing what we have with others, tending their comfort and needs, and providing an atmosphere of warmth and joy are ways of energizing and encouraging people. One does not have to be married to do this. Singles are just as capable of hospitality; in fact, it is healthy for them to extend this kind of cordiality as it gives them a chance to prepare for and serve others.

Hospitality is a Biblical mandate but often neglected in the pace of life. It requires sacrifice and a different attitude than "entertaining." It teaches a kind of openhandedness that is beneficial in relating to people. Someone who is stingy or protective of personal privacy will have a more difficult time in interaction with others or exhibiting care. Hospitality enables us to energize people right where we live.

5. Stewardship

Four basic areas require stewardship and they demonstrate much about a person.

◆ Time

A precious commodity, we are told in Scripture to "redeem the time" and make the most of our opportunities (Eph. 5:16). Someone who desires to equip others will have actual allotted time for ministry. This means saving space in one's regular schedule for getting together with people for the purpose of instruction, fellowship and mutual edification.

◆ Talents

Having a "sane estimation" of one's abilities (Rom. 12:3) is necessary to use the God-given natural capabilities and spiritual gifts effectively. When recognized as tools from God, they are offered to Him for His use. Proper stewardship of these talents will promote humility and also prevent "spinning the wheels" in an area where a person is not gifted.

◆ Money

Being "entrusted with the true riches" of the kingdom (Luke 16:11) is a by-product of having finances in order. There should be a giving of personal income to support the work of the Lord both locally and beyond; however, the true test of stewardship is often found in what is left over after the tithe is given. If there is burdensome indebtedness, measures should be taken to get out from underneath that kind of load. Many believers find themselves strapped financially, and it is a constant preoccupation as well as a limitation.

♦ RELATIONSHIPS

Having a high view of humanity (image-bearers of God) will generate a high view of relationships as well, whether it be non-believing family members, neighbors and friends, or fellow believers in the body of Christ. Relationships are a treasure and an investment, and wise stewardship of them is required in order that they can be cultivated, developed and enjoyed. Follow-up on conversations, research to answer questions, notes of encouragement, chatting over lunch, theological bull sessions, engaging in sports, joint vacations, long-term comfort in tragedy, participation in graduations, weddings, funerals and other special events all demonstrate good stewardship.

There is also the factor of mutual ministry in relationships, which calls for respecting fellow workers in their areas of giftedness. Honoring the positions and work of others in the church will bring about harmony andcohesiveness in the body of Christ if good stewardship is exercised in recognizing these various places of ministry.

6. WORLD CHRISTIAN

God's enterprise involves the world. In guiding others, it would seem important that an equipper not be insulated or isolated. Having an understanding that reflects a belief that the kingdom of God is bigger than one's own small world is important. This would mean being able to look beyond one's own circumstances to a broader picture, and being concerned about God's work around the world. Such an outlook would aid in guiding others with a balanced perspective of local and world ministry. Responding to Christ's great commission in the proper sense helps avoid parochialism. He *could* call a person to anywhere in the world.

7. Defined Ministry

As time goes by, any disciple of Christ should have a clearer definition of what his personal ministry ought to be. This would come through experimentation in the corporate life of the church in the various areas of service available. If one is serious about having a defined ministry, it is simply necessary to do an assortment of things, even if it results in frustration or failure. In fact, failure often helps define a person's gifting. Many believers have been surprised to discover capabilities and enjoyment in working with infants and toddlers, teens, or older saints. Teaching a Sunday School class has brought many abilities to the fore, or helping with the many areas of physical service. It is delightful to see people recognize their gifts and gain a clearer picture of their calling. It is also a blessing to be able to confidently refer others to these people, knowing they will receive the guidance needed.

◊   ◊   ◊   ◊   ◊

Each of these areas could be a seminar in itself. Although large subjects, they are marks of a maturing believer and are borne out of the general admonitions in scripture. Each of us is in process in these areas. No one has "arrived." The equipper should be far enough along in these qualities that a genuine, demonstrative faith is recognized by others. In turn, after a person has been through a discipling process, this could be used as an evaluation of weak and strong points to determine if further specific training is needed.

Chapter VIII

ONE-ON-ONE VERSUS GROUP DISCIPLESHIP

Many interesting discussions have transpired over the strengths and weaknesses of different methods used in disciplemaking. There are several variables to consider, of course, which will not be enumerated here, but I merely want to make some observations on the modes of one-on-one discipleship and group discipleship. There is a time and place for both styles.

THE ONE-ON-ONE METHOD

1. Personal Evangelism

One-on-one discipleship seems to occur most often when the new believer has been brought to faith in Christ by the discipler. If there is a prior relationship, it is very natural for discipling to take place within that relationship. The human agent responsible for the new birth should also accept the privilege and obligation for the growth. If he is unable to meet regularly with the new believer for the purpose of instruction, then the new believer should be referred to someone who can.

2. Exceptional Circumstances

There are other scenarios where someone might request a one-on-one situation. Some examples would be: a person's erratic travel schedule with work that prevents a regular meeting time; a college student's semester schedule that would make campus group meetings impossible; a short-term "crash course" with someone because of an impending move; an illness that keeps a person housebound; imprisonment; a long confinement in the hospital, or a situation where a parent is bound by a special-needs child. When a person is desirous of being discipled but his circumstances prevent meeting with a group, the one-on-one method seems appropriate and even necessary. Exceptional circumstances would mandate one-on-one discipling.

WARNING: Individualism

When someone requests a one-on-one commitment because of the privatization so common in the culture today, the request should not be considered. People who want to lead privatized lives with no one interfering with their plans and doing what they want to do when they want to do it, reek of individualism, and are the very people who need to be in a group. Certainly one of the features of discipling people today is acquainting them with the beauty of the body of Christ, the necessity of being membered with other believers, learning to talk through differences and accepting the accountability that the group brings. No one should be an isolated individual, unconnected from the community of believers. Disciplers should not accommodate the cultural attitudes that govern people and are contrary to scripture. Part of the training is to show the fallacy of the ultra-individualism of the day.

If a person is sincere about learning but thinks the social chit-chat of a group would be a distraction or even a time-waster, those expectations can be discussed and honored. Like-minded people could be put together so that the purpose of the group can be accomplished and the experience be satisfying to all involved.

PERSONAL EXAMPLE OF ONE-ON-ONE

Through personal experience with one-on-one discipling and observation of others, I recommend that one-on-one be short-term, and that wherever possible, the person be referred to a group. Some years ago, I was thrilled when a neighbor told me she had prayed (alone at home) to become a Christian. When she also mentioned that she came to that decision by watching our family, I felt an obligation to follow up on her profession of faith. She and her husband were not in a church and there were no other Christians in her life, so after some weeks, I asked if she would be interested in getting together to discuss the Christian faith. Because I was already leading a discipleship group, my teenage children were active in sports and music, and there were other commitments that took my time, I suggested a short-term study using Campus Crusades's "Transferable Concepts," mainly to get her grounded in her new-found belief. So one morning a week, after my children left for school and her two preschoolers were fed and happy, I ran next door for an hour and we discussed "How To Be Sure You Are A Christian."

It was a profitable time, but as the weeks went by, I sensed she needed others who could make our discussions more interesting and less threatening for her. She needed lots of affirmation and encouragement. She also viewed me as so far ahead in knowledge that my questions were often answered with, "This is probably a really stupid answer, but…" She refused to ever consider praying out loud because it just wasn't "her." Even though the study was basically doctrinal, social issues would come up and she reasoned her position on sex before marriage and abortion ("one or two abortions is okay, but more than that would be wrong") as a generational difference between us. She was "taught to make up my own mind on these things." The Bible still had little authority in her life.

After we completed the first booklet, I suggested she join a short-term Bible study that had just begun for the summer months. There were six in the group, mostly her age with young children, and I sat in on a few sessions. It was a lively, talkative group, and she felt comfortable with the women. When someone suggested they close the meeting with each person saying a sentence prayer, she joined in and thanked the Lord for one thing. It was a beginning. My hopes were that after awhile, she would become part of a discipleship group, but a move took them out of the area, and there has been no evidence of continued growth in her life. However, I'm thankful for the time we had together and for the experience itself, which was enlightening to me.

3. Strengths and Weaknesses of the Leader

Hopefully, the strengths of the discipler will "rub off" in a one-on-one situation…that the person being discipled will pick up on the fine qualities in the leader's life. Because of the intimacy in a personal life-on-life arrangement, there is a good chance for that. The downside is that the weaknesses of the discipler can also be passed on. This was depicted for me in an example where a newcomer to our church became a believer and was immediately taken under the wing of an older woman who knew the Bible and could teach well. The weakness of the older woman was that she had a sarcastic side to her, was not careful when speaking of her husband and children, and freely expressed skepticism about a number of areas in the church and community. I began to hear the same kind of remarks coming from the new Christian, who admired the older woman so much that she probably thought it was acceptable to speak that way. With no one else in the group, the remarks couldn't be tempered or challenged.

We often are blind to our own weaknesses and deficiencies. We are not mature in every area. We emphasize some things strongly and let other matters slide. Having two or more people in a group provides a protection and accountability for all involved. As the trust level rises in a group, some of these personal habits or quirks can be addressed and even confronted. Also, it is possible, when there are only two people, that one of them can be misunderstood and misquoted. We don't always hear things correctly or give a thorough explanation of something we are discussing, causing a misunderstanding. This can create quite a furor if the matter is serious enough. When there are no other witnesses, it's "her word against mine." Although this is rare, I have seen it happen. Most of the time, the matter can be cleared up quickly with a proper explanation of what was said. Sometimes though, the relational recovery takes awhile if feelings were hurt.

4. Time Efficiency

One final thought on why the one-on-one arrangement is less desirable than the group. It is a better use of time to disciple more than one person. As previously described, disciplemaking is a long-term commitment to a few. Considering the amount of time, energy and effort involved, it is more profitable to take several persons at once. For me, it is difficult enough limiting myself to just four, when there are so many others who could be included. Time is such a precious commodity and we all have to learn to use it wisely.

In summary, I would encourage meeting with a small group over one-on-one; however, at the same time, I would not want to discredit the meaningful exchanges and time spent in one-on-one situations. There is a sweetness and intimacy that many enjoy when only two people are present. Those dynamics are significant, and I do not mean to diminish their importance, but suggest that discretion be used in this approach.

Disciplemaking

THE GROUP METHOD

Speaking now from personal experience, throughout the years, discipleship has held much variety for me… from different group sizes, ages, personalities and meeting times to different curriculum. Although "variety is the spice of life," there are some ingredients that just work better than others and rarely do I vary them anymore. The syllabus is fairly set, even though the curriculum itself changes somewhat depending on who is in the group. I've always had weekly meetings, but the variation has come with each group on the agreed-upon hours of that meeting. The minimum time I can do is two hours. Anything less is not enough. Usually, the meetings last from 9:00 a.m.-12:00 p.m., and the dear women in my group arrange their schedule to commit to that. I had one group that was so intensely into the material and discussions, that we often went from 9:00-1:00. None of them had a pressing afternoon commitment, so we just stayed together and had the luxury of expanding and elaborating on the subject at hand. (It was that group that encouraged me to broaden the apologetic aspect of the material. No wonder.)

There are always a variety of personalities, and that is very important because personalities provide the atmosphere. The quick wits balance out the slower thinkers, and the "straight-shooters" balance out those who speak cautiously and carefully. The hearty laughs balance out the quiet smiles, and the outgoing balance out the unassertive. Groups are melting pots of personalities, and it is part of the learning process to adapt, adjust and enjoy the variety.

Having had various group sizes, from two to six, I've settled comfortably on four plus myself. Praying for four women and being involved with them beyond the weekly meeting, is about what I can handle, considering my other commitments. If there are more than four, I have found that we don't get through the material, spend time in prayer, or worship together like we should. Sometimes, it is healthy just to chat about current events, especially if their lives have been directly affected. Because I often have the women write papers on a subject and teach the material to the group, it's difficult to get around to all of them in one morning if there are more than four. And because we do dinner parties in each other's homes with our husbands (is this really the most important reason?), 10 people is a manageable number.

I have had 25-year age spans in my group and that works fine, depending on the women. Some have been believers for many years and some for only a few, and that also works well, depending on the women. When there is an agreed-upon goal and purpose, and the material is stimulating enough for all, everyone can enjoy the process. Many women have told me they do not want to be in a group with just peers, but find an intergenerational dynamic to be more interesting, and even helpful. I do not look at age as much as teachability, so the age differences often do not register with me until our first get-acquainted session. As it turned out, one group was all within five years of each other, but their children were in completely different stages.

As I get older, I am more inclined to take women who are a little older. Although I truly love the young women in their early 20's, I desire for the 30 to 40-year-old disciplers to invite them into their groups, so as difficult as it is not to ask them, I let other women have the privilege. I have found that many women in their 40's and 50's have never been discipled, and many of them desire that kind of experience so they, in turn, can teach others.

Obviously I believe in the older-teaching-the-younger principle. This is played out especially when talking about child-raising and other family matters. It helps tremendously if the discipler has been down that road first and can encourage from experience rather than from theory. Because some women have postponed childbearing until their late 30's, in some cases the discipler is younger than the one she is discipling, but her children are quite a bit older than the disciple's children. If the discipler is also older in Christ, it would work for the younger to teach the older, if the older has a teachable spirit and can learn from her. There are variables on the older/younger principle, but it is a scriptural guideline that has been given to us, and for the most part, it works best.

Can a woman disciple others when she herself has never been discipled? As my preface stated, I was that woman. I was limited because that experience had never been mine. I did not recognize the need to nurture others because I had never been taken under someone's wing. I did not know what to do when the opportunity to disciple came my way, because I had never been through the process myself. I had to learn about group dynamics, individual's expectations, clashing personalities, structure and flexibility all through the doing of it. All of that could have been a working knowledge had I learned those things by participating in a discipleship group. But our sovereign Lord didn't have that planned for me, so it became a matter of obedience to His command. Yes, a person can disciple others without having had the experience herself. It always comes down to obeying what Christ asked us to do. But it is a special bonus to have had a good discipling experience. Not only is there a comprehension of material to be used, but a knowledge of what it takes to work with people. What a blessing it is to pass on what was passed to you!

CHAPTER IX

THE SELECTION PROCESS

Selection involves choice and a sense of recruitment, both of which are necessary to forming a group. Because disciples are not mass-produced, the number of individuals in one group must be few, making the issue of selection significant. For the leader of the group, committing a large amount of time to these few also emphasizes the vital nature of careful selection. And because the ultimate goal of the discipling process is reproduction, those few should at least have a heart for duplicating the process.

It appears that one becomes a discipler through two means: evangelization and the concept of the older believer teaching the younger believer (the "Titus II principle").

1. EVANGELIZATION

This is the ideal. Recruiting people to the kingdom of God and starting "from scratch" is the optimal goal of the Christian. This is truly fulfilling Christ's commission: "go and make disciples." There is nothing more rewarding or gratifying than bringing a person to faith in Christ and being involved in the development of that new believer. Pre-evangelism and conversion are the beginning of the discipleship process. When this happens, there is more of an "obligation awareness" than "selection awareness" because the new believer is right there, a "babe" in the faith, ready to be nurtured.

The person responsible for the birth is the person most likely to care for the new believer.

In many countries around the world, the church is growing primarily through evangelism. In fact, the new births outnumber the nurturers to such a degree, that there is an urgency in discipleship. The new converts are vulnerable to counterfeits, the cults, and other deviations of the true faith unless mature believers can train them properly. Because many of these people are coming to Christ out of great need and lack of privilege so common to Americans, there is a vitality and genuineness to their faith that makes them ripe for discipling. There is also great motivation to equip everyone in the church because everyone is needed in the instruction of the new professing believers.

In America, where many churches grow more by the "migratory flock" rather than by new birth, evangelicals are often passive in "sharing their faith" because the church gives the impression that it is doing okay without that emphasis. However, evangelism does occur (whether it be one-on-one, group, or mass crusade), and for those who do bring others to faith in Christ, they know that nothing equals the delight of new birth and subsequent growth.

2. OLDER BELIEVERS TEACHING YOUNGER BELIEVERS

Rather than going outside the community of believers, engaging in evangelism and follow-up, this is tapping the potential that already exists within the church and bringing those believers to maturity. Such potential also exists in the work place, college campus, neighborhood, etc. where believers are present. If a church has experienced numerical growth because people have migrated from other congregations (especially if those congregations are characterized by liberal theology, lack of Bible teaching or a distorted view of the Christian walk), there probably is much opportunity for proper discipleship. Or perhaps there are a number of new believers who are fresh in their faith or those who never received suitable nourishment and remain in spiritual infancy. In most churches, there are many who desire discipleship, or if they don't know what it is, need it anyway.

The local church is an ideal environment for discipling others. Christopher Adsit, in his book, *Personal Disciplemaking*, calls the church, "the divine incubator" (chap. 4). The work of the disciplemaker is reinforced in the local church (or at least it should be) so that he alone does not bear the weight of nurturing an individual. Regular contact and fellowship with other believers provides the "incubator" where development is encouraged.

In spite of commendable efforts on campus, many parachurch organizations have experienced disappointing results once the on-campus discipling of students is terminated by graduation and the student moves on. If students haven't been "plugged in" to a local church, or see the importance of that, their discipling has been anemic and short-sighted. The church is God's plan for *all* believers.

The example of Jesus and the admonitions of Paul applies to discipleship within the community of believers. Gathering a group together and leading them so they will not only understand the Christian life but be able to live it successfully, is the objective. This is teaching others so they in turn can teach others. Titus 2 is precise about the older teaching the younger, but even in the other admonitions of Paul that seems to be the pattern. This is where the selection process comes in. Accessing the pool of believers in a local body presents the challenge and privilege of recruitment.

TO ASK OR NOT TO ASK

There are two approaches in forming a discipleship group: to be asked, or to ask. It is an honor as well as humbling *to be asked* by someone to disciple them. It usually means the desire for such nurturing is strong, there is an obvious lack or need, and they have been influenced by your example. It is equally humbling *to ask* someone to place himself or herself under your tutelage. It involves courage, vision, and prayer to approach an individual with the proposal of enlisting in your discipleship group. Either approach… to ask or to be asked…is valid. I personally do not see one as more ideal than the other.

When you are asked by someone to disciple him or her, it does not automatically mean that you should do it. The fit may not be good. It could be that the person does not know anyone else who leads discipleship groups, so you are their only choice. Or perhaps a friend is in such a group and it sounds interesting. If there is not a full understanding of what discipleship means, there could be any number of reasons why a person would ask you to disciple them. There have been times when I have referred a woman to another discipler who would be a better match. This might involve whether or not the woman is a new or older believer, the stage of life she is in (caring for infants or an empty-nester), personal problems (depression, divorce, death of spouse, etc.), or other such matters. There have been times when I really wanted to accommodate the person who asked to be in my group, but the time was not right. Often, they are willing to wait a couple of years, especially if it means re-arranging the commitments in their life in preparation for the group. Even though it is an honor to be asked, it presents some challenges. If the match is not good or the time right, there is then the obligation of making certain the person is cared for. This can be frustrating if the disciplers are few in number or if their groups are full. It is agonizing to see an "eager beaver" put on hold because there are no disciplers.

Because a person has not asked to be discipled does not mean the desire is not there. Most likely, they just have not considered it, do not know what it is, or do not know who would be willing to disciple them. These are the people who should be asked, and they usually respond positively. To ask means you are recruiting. Even though "recruitment" has a military or official sound to it, the word itself is a good one. It simply means taking the initiative in the selection process. It means there is choice involved in putting a group together. The seasoned discipler knows that these kinds of decisions are critical. One experienced discipler said to me recently: "Selection is everything!" What does this mean? What do you look for when recruiting prospective members of a group?

Desired qualifications in Those Recruited

I asked several discipleship group leaders to write down what they look for, and here is a summarized list of qualifications they deem necessary.

- Love for the Lord
- Teachable spirit
- Desire to delve deeply
- Willing to be vulnerable
- Willing to be accountable
- Desire to grow
- Eager to learn
- An appetite
- Willing to give significant effort to the process
- Seeker of truth
- Time
- Willing to be outside one's own little world
- Available for the duration of the time commitment

These characteristics could be condensed into a few main categories. In her book, *Discipling One Another*, Ann Ortland lists three main qualifications. I agree wholeheartedly with these and have found that all three need to be present simultaneously. A person must be:

1. Available

One should be loose enough from the world's system to commit to such an endeavor and loose enough in schedule to give significant effort to the discipling process. If a person's life is packed, our own conscience should not permit us to add to that. I have had women assure me that they could "squeeze it in," or that they were capable of "handling a lot." For most women, the choices they must face are all good choices. Eliminating something that is good in order to do something else that's good is very difficult, especially when they are told that "you can have it all." There have been instances when I did not want to see a woman give up an important commitment in order to join my group, so we decided upon a plan whereby she could release herself from that responsibility over time, or change another obligation.

2. Teachable

One has to be reminded that "disciple" means "learner." There has to be a willingness and desire to learn. Sometimes a great personality can camouflage a resisting spirit or a mindset that just is not open to receive. Unfortunately, an unteachable spirit is often more typical of someone who has known the Lord for awhile than of the new Christian. It is a difficult group dynamic when someone delights in being the "answer man" and is always instructing others. If there is an attitude of "having arrived," a yellow flag should go up in considering such a candidate for the group. Likewise, the new believer is not teachable if she delights in arguing her position, and there is an unwillingness to release a secular mindset in order to learn "the mind of Christ." Some preliminary work needs to be done before such a person can be a true "learner."

3. Eager --- or "have heart" (Ortland)

Keenness for the discipling process is a wonderful quality, sometimes a result of the Holy Spirit's work in an individual, sometimes a result of understanding what discipleship is all about and sometimes a response to the opportunity for deeper learning. Enthusiasm makes a person an absolute delight in the group, and that excitement is contagious. More than brilliance or education, eagerness is the desired quality. If a person has half-heartedly consented to the discipling process, or if there is a lackluster compliance to someone's encouragement to be discipled, those attitudes can be spoilers for everyone involved.

I have learned (sometimes painfully) that all three qualities need to exist in someone interested in being discipled. A woman can be eager and available, but if she is not teachable, there will be discouragement and frustration ahead for the discipler. A woman can be teachable and eager, but if she is not available, there will be irregularity in attendance, unfinished assignments and frequent excuses for lack of participation. A woman can be teachable and available, but if she is not eager, it will be like tugging on the reins and inventing ways of stirring excitement.

There has to be an individual assessment in the selection process. These three characteristics provide a unified foundation for the group. When the leader knows that each person possesses these qualities, the framework for a fruitful group is squarely in place.

The Exclusive Nature of Selection

Just a word about the fact that when some are selected, it means others are not. Because discipleship clusters work best when they are small, there is an exclusivity to this pursuit. And once the group is formed, it is limited to those few for the designated period of time. When a disciplemaking ministry within the church is first initiated, people might misunderstand the exclusive nature of this activity and suspect it of being cliquish and feel rejected. Women, especially, seem sensitive to being "left out" of something that others are doing. Because of the long-term nature of discipleship groups in our own church, they function without a lot of publicity or recognition, yet, word does get around that they are operating. It has been our experience that in time, people do understand the nature of this pursuit because they see the reproductive cycle, and of course, more are included as the years go by. In the meantime, loving explanations can be given. In fact, it is a good way to educate people on the necessity and importance of discipleship.

The exclusive nature of selection is painful to the discipler as well, because there are always more people desiring discipleship than can be taken. Throughout the years, this has become easier for me to accept, but it is still agonizing not to be able to include those who are ripe for the process. When our daughter and her husband returned from China with their adopted 10-month old girl, their joy was tempered by the fact that so many orphans remained. Selecting one, when there were many left, was difficult, yet what they did was right and good. Yes, there is an exclusive side to selection, but once again, I am encouraged by the example of Jesus and the fact that he restricted His group to twelve, when there undoubtedly could have been many more. If anyone could have led a larger group effectively, it would have been Jesus.

Selection is Important to Group Dynamics

If discipling more than one person at a time, the discipler should also consider the compatibility of the individuals involved. There is no perfect, foolproof way of covering all the angles in putting people together, but if there are glaring differences, one should not try to force people together. An outspoken older Christian could completely overpower and intimidate a younger new believer. If a person is very relational and hopes discipleship will involve lots of personal sharing and intimacy, and another person is expecting academia with outlines and research, the leader will have quite a juggling act to perform. When someone wants to spend much time in prayer and another wants to socialize more, there could be conflict in the group. Obviously, some of those expectations can be dealt with when the objectives of the process are discussed before someone even commits to joining. This would include going over the curriculum, the goals of the leader, and a sketch of how the meetings will run. However, there really is no way to know people well enough to avoid the unexpected snags in group dynamics.

That is why the selection process takes much prayer and consideration. There are times when I have asked others to pray for me as I put my group together. Occasionally, when the group is partially formed, I have consulted with trusted advisors on who would fit well with those in the group. Sometimes a group is formed easily and other times it takes considerable effort. An illustration of the importance of selection is a quilting project. After the design is chosen, for me, the most critical part of the quilt is the initial step of fabric selection. Deciding what colors will work well together is crucial to the design and final outcome of the quilt. And because the quilt is handled and worked on over a long period of time, it is nice to enjoy the colors and not weary of them.

In discussion with other group leaders on the issue of selection, some have expressed that a prior relationship is necessary. Discipleship would seem natural and genuine if the discipler and disciple knew each other well. It certainly is preferable for discipleship to be a natural outflow of an existing relationship. When potential disciplers say they don't know who to disciple and no one has asked them, the obvious answer is to initiate friendships and relationships with other women. It doesn't have to be an intense relationship or longstanding, but it does help to know others well enough to begin a conversation about discipleship. (This all appears to be more important to women than men. Men seem less concerned about who will be in a group and just what the procedure will be. Relational issues are crucial to women, sometimes to a fault.)

But even a prior relationship is no guarantee that there will be no surprises. I have asked people who I thought I knew well to be in my group, and then discovered much about them that I never knew (sometimes to my delight and sometimes to my sadness). I've not hesitated to ask women to consider my group who I did not know well, but through observation, sensed they were ready for this kind of commitment. I've not found it necessary that all the group members know each other either. In fact, one of the joys of these groups is the new relationships that are solidly formed. Much of the group dynamic depends on the leader, how clearly she has related the goals and expectations of the process and how she handles the weekly meetings. Through experience, she gets better at "reading" people, what to spend more time doing (or less), and how to balance the fun and seriousness of the times together. Personally, my discipleship groups are such a joy to me, and so much fun, that I do not worry much about the potential for difficult dynamics. Besides, the Holy Spirit is very good at melding a group together and exceeding any expectations I might have.

Chapter X

REPRODUCTION

A Vision for Multiplication

Jesus Christ was God in the form of man. Although He relinquished the independent use of His divine attributes when He humbled Himself and took on an earthly body, He was still God, with a divine and human nature co-existing. He was a perfect human with great capabilities. During His years of public ministry, He was not married, did not raise children, did not operate a business, did not coach little league or serve on the school board. He was completely free to give Himself to the ministry. Yet with all of these advantages, He believed He could only effectively train 12 men. Surely, with His abilities He could have successfully handled 50 or more! The reproductive factor would have been more broad-based and impressive. But He invested His efforts in a few, having a vision for multiplication. The example of Jesus is striking because it emphasizes that disciples cannot be mass-produced. If reproduction is to occur, then the effort needs to be put into the quality of the training, not numbers.

There is an interesting scenario found in II Cor. 2:12-13, where Paul had a marvelous opportunity to preach in Troas. The door was wide open and apparently many were waiting to hear him. Paul was not only a gifted speaker but was commissioned by the Lord to preach the Gospel. Yet, he turned down the opportunity because he "had no rest in his spirit" since he didn't know where Titus was. He was so concerned, that he turned his back on an open door and a potentially big event to find his co-worker. It appears that Paul was more concerned about one man than the masses. But Paul knew that in training Titus, he would double the effectiveness of his ministry. In one man, there was more potential for multiplication than in the crowd of listeners.

Paul felt the same way about Timothy, and in the Pastoral Epistles we are impacted by the exhortations and encouragements Paul gives this son in the faith. Much was at stake in Paul's investment in Titus and Timothy. The training of these two was critical in the multiplication of future disciples who would take the gospel to even greater extents.

It is also interesting that Philip was whisked away from a fruitful campaign in Samaria so that he could speak with one man…an Ethiopian from a foreign land. The Lord certainly knew that Philip could multiply his ministry substantially, and in a faraway place, if the Ethiopian became the key person in reaching his country. Scenarios like these give the impression that although dealing with the masses is important, one or two individuals *really* matter if there's to be healthy reproduction.

Any valid ministry we are occupied with ought to be reproductive. When an endeavor lives and dies with us, we have not properly trained others to carry on. Sometimes the vision and gifts of others can develop the effort to a greater degree than we could ever take it. Paul could have been completely absorbed in evangelizing and teaching. He was very good at it. For such a brilliant man, so educated and dynamic, discipling a few men might have been tedious and unglamorous for him, yet it was a top priority. If we are truly interested in reproducing, then training others needs to be uppermost in our minds.

It takes a discipler to make disciples. Perhaps one reason why this endeavor has been ignored by the church is that it is not a rapid multiplication, and the process itself is slow and costly. Today, when quick results are preferred, few are attracted to a tedious effort that may or may not produce the desired outcome. Even Jesus did not have 100% reproduction with His twelve. The fact that Judas fell away is sad, yet it is a realistic picture of what happens when working with people. There are no guarantees that the discipling effort will secure a person's walk with the Lord from that time forward and that there will be no failures. Yet it is the thing Christ asked us to do.

Teaching others so *they* can teach others is the vision of reproduction. The disciplemaker should have this end in sight when he begins the process with a small cluster of disciples. The disciples should also understand that this is the desired end result…that the process really is not complete until the turn-around has been made. Because discipleship groups become close-knit and usually enjoy each other and the process immensely, the aim of reproduction can become dim. The group itself becomes the focus and no one is thinking much beyond the enjoyment of meeting together week after week. And perhaps that is as it should be. But every now and then, it would not hurt for the leader to give gentle reminders such as: "Now, when you teach this unit to your own group…" or "Depending on who you are discipling, you might want to change how we handled this area…" Such remarks bring back to mind the objective of reproduction.

Is the Great Commission for Everybody?

The issue of reproduction hinges to a great extent on a person's view of Matt. 28:19-20. Historically, the church has believed that Christ's commission found in these verses is for **all** believers, not just the original Twelve. If this is true, and if we really believe that, then all followers of Christ can be disciplemakers. Regardless of our talents and gifts, all women and all men should be fulfilling His command.

"Making disciples" transcends our personalities, gifts, talents, and even callings. It must be then, that everyone has the ability to disciple someone. That's encouraging news. No matter a person's vocation, he can be a disciplemaker. In fact, in many cases, the vocation itself provides a platform.

It seems that many Christians find this hard to take and somehow exempt themselves from Christ's command. It is true that some Biblical commands are easier to accept than others, depending on our personalities. To be "tenderhearted and forgiving" might come easily for a person whose obvious gift is mercy, but for a charger whose administrative skills make him think task before people, it might come harder. To "pray without ceasing" might be a delight for the believer gifted in faith and who can trust God for anything, but for the doer who takes pleasure in service, finding the time to pray will be more challenging. The command, "children, obey your parents" is fairly natural for the compliant child, but for the strong-willed, it comes after much resistance. To "be content with what you have" is not too difficult for the person who enjoys simplicity and an uncluttered lifestyle, but for the entrepreneur whose satisfaction is in the developing, it might be foreign language. "Go and make disciples" might be more comfortable for a natural leader who has initiative and drive, but for the reticent who concentrates on personal inadequacies, it will require extra courage.

Feelings of Inadequacy

When Jesus commissioned His disciples, they were not experienced disciplers themselves; in fact, they barely understood His teachings. It is obvious they were still in the dark on a number of issues and would remain so until the Holy Spirit enlightened them. These were not men who had graduated with flying colors and could be fully trusted. It was only a few days before when Peter confessed to Christ that he did not love Him as he should (John 21:15-17). Things were not perfect with this group. They still had much to learn, and they must have been acutely aware of their inadequacies.

One of the most common comments I have heard from women who have been through a discipling process and then hesitate to reproduce is: "I don't think I can do this myself. I still feel so inadequate." This used to bother me a great deal, and almost always, I faulted the discipling process, thinking that something got left out, the teaching was deficient, or there wasn't a clear understanding of the ultimate goal. But then one day it dawned on me that this is a natural response on the part of one who has never discipled others. Perhaps it's been the normal reaction of disciples throughout history. It's the way it should be, for the adequacy is developed in the doing. Over time, the competence and capability materializes, not before the doing.

Two months before our first child was born, there wasn't much evidence in our house that we were about to have a baby. Finances were tight, and except for a crib, we had purchased nothing. Then one evening, the church threw a baby shower for us, and we got everything we needed and more. It was so exciting to receive all those wonderful gifts! We put everything in our living room, and for days, I kept looking at the items, touching the clothes, winding the swing, smiling at the toys, and knowing I now had the equipment necessary to care for a baby.

But I still felt inadequate about becoming a mother. What would it be like? How would I know what to do? Would it be really difficult? What if I botched things royally? I now had all the equipment, but it didn't assure me that I would be a good mother. I was trying to feel adequate for a task I had yet to perform. I wanted to be confident in something that was never before experienced.

When our daughter, Gina, was born a few weeks later, the doing began, and with the doing came the capability, the satisfaction and the confidence. Mistakes were made. There were sleepless nights and moments when I was not sure what to do, but an adequacy for the task was developed. Three years later, when Ryan was born, I did not have those first-time questions or fears. Knowing this child would be different and present new challenges did not frighten me. I was up to the task, no matter what lay ahead.

I liken this to the new disciplemaker. She's taken a "class" on how to do it. She's seen it done. With the material, she's received the equipment. But she won't feel self-assured, knowledgeable enough or adequate enough until she does it herself. Assurance comes with the doing. And the second time around, there will be an even greater confidence because the skill is developing.

Reasons Given for Lack of Reproduction

The cycle of discipleship…teaching others so they will teach others… is critical to the long-term success of the endeavor. It can be likened to passing the baton in a relay race. At track meets, I have always enjoyed watching the relay because it involves several athletes who run a leg of the long race individually, but at a critical moment, the baton is passed between two of them. That is the instant of tension, and I usually hold my breath at that point. The race lives or dies with a good transfer. If the baton is dropped, the race is in jeopardy.

I have had several discussions with others committed to discipleship on why the baton gets dropped. Over the years, many reasons have been given why women are not involved in discipling others. Here are some:

- ✧ Viewing discipleship as an option, rather than a command
- ✧ Overextended in commitments

- Low confidence level
- Didn't understand the reproductive factor before consenting to discipleship
- Involvement with other ministries
- Homeschooling
- Not enough knowledge
- Family commitments, especially sports
- The "tyranny of the urgent"
- Fear of failure
- The costs of time, energy and relationships seem too great
- Still having a mindset of wanting to receive rather than giving back
- Some seasons in life are more conducive than others to this process
- Apathy
- Knowing who to disciple
- Unwilling to make a regular, long-term commitment

These reasons, some positive and some negative, are understandable and I have discussed them at length with other disciplers. Some of the reasons can be easily dealt with; others are difficult to resolve. When women do not "feel ready" to duplicate the process and put it off, I have observed that it rarely happens down the road. Life always fills up with other commitments that then become the priority. Over the years, I have watched a growing trend among women to want to receive rather than give. The time invested in them was taken lightly, and now they are on to other Bible studies where they can once again receive. All of the above reasons have generated much thought, prayer and discussion. In the end, it often comes down to obeying what Christ commanded us to do.

There are many ways to influence others for the good, to encourage growth and enable people to strengthen their beliefs. Usually there are a variety of ministries within the local church that people can engage in so there is the satisfaction of serving the Lord and "building the body." Workers often find their niche in a particular area and are effective and appreciated greatly for what they do. Women who come out of discipleship groups usually have a maturity in their walk as well as an understanding of people that is beneficial to these areas of service. They add depth to the local church.

Having watched women for years and listened to them explain the "whys" of their involvements, I still cannot get around Christ's command to "go and make disciples." Knowing from personal experience what it is like to balance other valid ministries and family life with disciplemaking, and being very familiar with the frustration of not fully developing other areas of interest because of the time and energy involved, and struggling with the dilemma of not being available for other relationships, I am aware of the cost. And contrary to what some might think, there is no season in life where disciplemaking is easy and without its challenges.

But there is no greater satisfaction in life than to reproduce in other people what God has taught me. There is such joy in the intimate relationships, the accountability, the study and in-depth discussions, that there is no substitute for it. Nothing has encouraged my own personal growth through the years more than discipling others. I have listened to motivational speakers, attended seminars and workshops, all designed to encourage personal spiritual maturity in believers. Everything I have heard is found in the disciplemaking endeavor. It is by far the best way to cultivate maturity, both in the discipler and those being discipled.

My admonition then, is straightforward. No matter what the involvement and how necessary the obligation, if it is not producing fruit in the life of someone else, it needs to be re-evaluated. If you are not "teaching others in order that they may teach others," you are not fulfilling the commands of scripture. Reproductive fruit should be the goal of every believer. If it is impossible to have a "formalized" group that meets regularly, you still need to be meeting with someone. Maybe it begins by lending an ear to someone's problems and developing a trust through that. After awhile, the relationship should be more than problem-centered, and the opportunity to nurture now exists. Maybe it is a co-worker who is anemic in the faith and only has the lunch hour for input from you. There are myriads of possibilities. Reproducing in the life of another individual what the Lord has taught you takes precedence over other involvements. No activity, busyness, commitment or other ministry should substitute for that.

Jesus said that He chose us to bear fruit (John 15:16) and that our fruit *should remain.* Certainly one of the applications of that would be the relay of truth, both objective and practical, in someone's life. When building on the foundation of Jesus Christ with "gold, silver and precious stones" (I Cor. 3:11-14), the proof of the work is that it *remain* (vs. 14). Investing in the life of an immortal being, a creation of God who will live eternally, is top priority. As C.S. Lewis so aptly said: "Nature is mortal; we shall outlive her. When all the suns and nebulae have passed away, each one of you will still be alive…There are no *ordinary* people. You have never talked to a mere mortal…It is immortals whom we joke with, marry, snub and exploit---immortal horrors or everlasting splendours" (from *The Weight of Glory*).

CHAPTER XI

KEEPING THE BIGGER PICTURE IN MIND

In our daily routine, whether it be homemaking, teaching school, work at the office, manual labor, pastoring a church or any other calling, there is the likelihood of losing sight of the bigger picture. With our "nose to the grindstone," the every-day schedule is our preoccuption and sometimes we forget *why* we are doing what we are doing. Or we forget *what* we hope to produce with all the energy expended day to day. Wise people have learned that a reminder of purpose and goals, as well as a re-evaluation of methods used is healthy. It keeps us on track and usually affirms what we are doing.

This is true in disciplemaking. Once the group has settled into a routine, it is easy to get absorbed in the weekly agenda and lose sight of the ultimate purpose. Because the times together are enjoyable with much to accomplish, the minutes pass quickly, and suddenly another meeting has ended and we're thinking about the following week. Here are aspects of the bigger picture to keep in mind.

1. THE CALL TO FOLLOW CHRIST

As stated earlier, the overarching call in life is to follow Christ. "Follow me" is the summons that all believers need to heed. These verses represent many that have to do with that summons:

Matt. 4:19: "And He said to them, *follow me* and I will make you fishers of men."

Matt. 16:24: "If anyone wishes to come after me, let him deny himself, and take up his cross and *follow me*."

John 10:27: "My sheep hear my voice, and I know them, and they *follow me*."

We are first and foremost disciples of His. As workers within His kingdom, we are recruiting people to a *life* of discipleship, not to a short-term class. Even though we are the human agency that will provide the environment for the learning, our fundamental concern is that these people be devoted followers of Christ. Therefore, we do not recruit to a program or a discipler, but to a *vision* of maturity in Christ. Keeping that in mind will help us stay on track as the many dynamics of a discipleship group are experienced. Should there be more prayer time? Should there be more personal sharing? If individuals confess to struggles with certain temptations, should there be an accountability reporting each week? Should there be more inductive study? Should there be more time given to developing apologetics? Is the material being digested and becoming part of the thinking mechanism? The overall concern is: how can we strengthen the response to the call of Christ?

2. THE CALL TO THE CHURCH

Jesus not only said, "Follow me," He said, "I will build my church" (Matt. 16:18). Every believer is "baptized into one body" (I Cor. 12:13) and membered with other believers. The context surrounding that statement in I Corinthians 12 is graphic, with the members being likened to parts of the body that cannot disown each other or pretend they have no need for each other. Membership in the universal body of Christ is "fleshed out" in the local church, and it is the duty of every Christian to align himself with a local community of believers. Part of the disciplemaking process should be to establish those who follow Christ in His plan for their lives. The church is His plan. The discipleship group is no substitute for the church.

The weakness of parachurch organizations has been at this point, and some of them have learned that being a disciple of Christ *for life* means that those who have been nurtured by their methods and strategies need to go beyond that and find long-term accountability in the body of Christ. It is true that many local churches have been disappointments to the follow-up process, especially to the work on college campuses. There is vitality and excitement in the growing faith of a new believer, but when scouting out local churches to sustain that, few can be found. In fact, some churches hinder the discipling that is occurring because of dead orthodoxy, legalism, liberalism or the entertainment factor so common in church services today. In spite of this discouragement, the importance of the church should still be part of the instruction. As soon as possible, those being discipled should join a local body where the Bible is taught and their Christian walk can be supported.

Discipleship groups will strengthen a local church and add a depth to its environment. Of course, that means that there is no contradictory teaching occurring within the groups. Without organizing the groups tightly, there has to be oversight to assure that the same doctrine is taught in all the groups with unified expectations of how to live the Christian life. The group leaders need accountability and agreement on the essentials. Each discipleship cluster will look a little different and go about the task in different ways, but every group is answerable to the eldership in the church, and of course, ultimately to the Lord.

Discipleship groups can be composed of a variety of people from a variety of churches (especially on the college campus), but it takes a strong leader to keep everyone on the essentials and not get sidetracked with denominational talk or the effects of liberal theology. If everyone is a sincere learner, this format can actually be quite stimulating and profitable. But if group members just want to argue their position, it could be frustrating and actually confusing, depending on the maturity of the leader.

Within a local community, it is preferable to have people from the same church in the same group. That is not a hard and fast rule, but it does avoid potential disagreements using "but my church does it this way" as an argument. Within a group, there usually is a lot of talk about what is happening in the local church, the teaching on Sunday, outreach efforts and people to pray about. With these shared experiences, there is a unity and oneness automatically expressed because of that common bond, as well as a feeling that the group is an extension of something bigger. If one person in the group attends another congregation, that kind of talk needs to be limited so she does not feel left out. Many times, my group has gathered for our weekly meeting and everyone wants to discuss further what happened last Sunday, either in the teaching or in worship. It is wonderful to be able to "chew it over" together, and those times have been valuable.

3. CONVICTION AND PERSPECTIVE

The cornerstones in the training to be disciples of Christ are conviction and perspective. They make all the difference in someone's life and determine whether a person will be self-motivated to obediently follow Christ or still rely heavily on someone else's direction. If a person lacks conviction and perspective they are not adequately trained.

"Conviction" --- "the state of being convinced" is what the dictionary says. Conviction connotes a firm persuasion, a certainty and steadfastness. Convictions come about by knowing the truth, and knowing what you believe and why you believe what you believe.

Being grounded in rich Biblical doctrine is the starting point as it provides the foundation for other areas. Having a good theology will enable someone to then develop convictions on womanhood, male and female relationships, family, child-raising, church government and a host of other practical issues. Convictions motivate and enable a person to be steady and unflinching in a secular, post-modern culture. They are like having an anchor in a turbulent sea.

One of the satisfying joys of parenting is watching your children develop their own convictions. They are doing what is right because *they* are motivated to do so, not because it is the expectation of Mom and Dad or the standard of the home. The goal of parental training is that the children will arrive at their own convictions.

In his helpful book, *Disciples Are Made Not Born*, Walt Henrichsen illustrates this point effectively by using a dishwashing scenario (Chap. 9). His wife had a certain method of washing dishes: glasses and silverware first, followed by plates and bowls, then pots and pans. Because he had no convictions about the order of dishwashing, just wanting to get the job done, he began with the pots and pans. She corrected him by explaining that in order to sterilize the utensils that had contact with the mouth, the glasses and silverware should be done first with the clean, hot sudsy water, followed by plates and finally the pots and pans (which can sterilize themselves while cooking). Understanding the principle, he developed convictions on dishwashing and did it that way even when his wife was not watching. Mindlessly practicing a certain method (or doing it just to please his wife) did not bring about the conviction. Understanding the principle did.

Understanding Biblical principles will form the understructure for all a person does. The *why* questions must be asked and answered if the principles are to be understood. Once they are, convictions will develop. People usually don't form convictions overnight. It takes patience, prayer and often much discussion to see people become fully persuaded and resolute about something. But it is worth every ounce of effort to see someone own his personal convictions.

"Perspective"--- "to look through and see clearly;" "the capacity to view things in their true relations or relative importance," says the dictionary. Perspective means a person has a comprehensive point of view and can see things more broadly. There is a sense of proportion in the way he does life. Perspective is seeing it like it is.

This involves having a proper view of God and a proper view of man. Although God is incomprehensible, He *is* knowable. His nature and character should be studied in order to have a correct view of the way His attributes function in unison and harmony simultaneously. (His love never operates without His holiness being present; His wrath is never expressed apart from His justice and righteousness.) Any good study of God will cause the student to have a large view of Him, and that is absolutely necessary to one's perspective. If God is small in our viewpoint, all situations or problems in life will be oversized.

Likewise, there needs to be a proper understanding of the origin and nature of man. The significance of bearing God's likeness, being the apex of His creation, the drastic effects of the fall, the propensity to sin, the brevity of life and being the object of God's constant love and faithfulness all give a balanced view of mankind. This counterbalances the contemporary approach of trying to build someone's self-esteem without giving the rich content that is foundational to a person's worth and dignity.

In addition to theology, perspective is developed by reading history and other great literature. A secular mindset judges everything by the here-and-now, and it will bring a limited view to current life if it is not balanced with hindsight (and foresight as well). A discipler should set the example in reading good books (certainly more than Christian self-help material). I'll never forget Edith Schaeffer's encouragement to me to always be reading something of at least 100 years before our time when people still had "clean sort of problems" and a basis upon which to solve life's dilemmas. Because of the tenacious nature of our present culture, it is easy to gauge everything by what currently *is*. It is ironic that with all the potential for information today through our technology and opportunities to travel, people still approach life and base their decisions primarily on the here-and-now.

When a person's perspective is out of focus, the temptation to commit sin can be great because he is not able to see the consequences of that sin. When someone's perspective is limited, their present problems can consume them if there isn't a proper view of God and man. Perspective has to do with your philosophy of life and the grid through which everything is viewed.

So, developing convictions and perspective should be a goal of the disciplemaker. It is a good exercise to have those being discipled to write down their convictions. Can they separate them from their opinions? Doctrinal convictions mean that you would probably give your life for something (such as Jesus being the *only* way to God) rather than compromise. Many in history have died for that reason. Watching people develop their convictions and the way they view life is stimulating and satisfying. It is wonderful to observe the Holy Spirit's work in an individual, "turn on the light bulbs," bring about authenticity, and provide a healthy perspective. He is the ultimate teacher and convincer of truth.

4. A VISION FOR REPRODUCTION

The same Jesus who said "follow me," also said "go and make disciples." If one command applies, so does the other. These statements are at the heart of Christ's public ministry on earth and have been recognized by believers throughout the ages as critical to the message of the Gospel. They both need to be in the foresight of the disciplemaker. To follow Christ is to hearken to His summons, recognize Him as Lord, and live under His authority. To go and make disciples, "teaching them to observe all" that Christ taught, is obedience to His plan for your life. This is the final goal of discipleship.

Because another chapter deals with the issue of reproduction, I will not repeat those thoughts. In practical terms, it is much different working with someone who has a heart for the Great Commission than someone who wants to be in a discipleship group just because it sounds interesting and more challenging than another Bible study. It excites me when someone asks to be in my group because they have people in mind they want to disciple. They pay close attention, not only to the curriculum itself, but to procedure and amount of time given to study, discussion, worship, sharing, etc. Notes are compiled and the material is being updated frequently because it will be the resourceful tool they use when they have their own group.

In reading books on disciplemaking, I have come across long lists of goals that the leader should have in mind for the members in his or her group. One book listed traits such as "a servant's heart," "reliable," "a heart for people," "leadership," etc. as objectives in discipleship, all admirable qualities. These are the four that I've listed:

- The Call to Follow Christ,
- The Call to the Church,
- Conviction and Perspective
- A Vision for Reproduction

Many aspirations of a discipler can be enumerated here, but for now, I offer these four areas for thought.

CHAPTER XII

THE WOMAN DISCIPLER

Although much of this chapter pertains to the woman discipler, many of the qualities listed would apply to men as well. In Chapter VII, the suggested distinctives of the equipper are enumerated, and since they are applicable to both men and women, they will not be repeated here. Some of those points will be expanded in this chapter because they are well suited to women, married or unmarried.

The woman discipler is in a privileged position of leadership. As a nurturer of women, she prepares for and guides her group in their course of study, prays for those in her care, evaluates the progress made, and is viewed as a role model and trusted example by those under her tutelage. It is humbling to have others want to spend this kind of time with you and submit to your plans for an extended period of time. It is remarkable that the Lord would place us in such a position of influence. Actually, it's astounding that He would use us at all! We should never cease to be amazed that God chooses to accomplish His purpose by using imperfect humans. He is content enough with our maturing process that He can allow for faltering steps and use us while we are growing up!

Titus 2:3-5 is the well-known passage that sets the pattern for women to teach other women. Specific qualities are highlighted in those verses, many having to do with the home. Obviously, in order for the older women to teach the younger, those qualities would have to be marks of the older woman's life so she can teach by word and example. Titus 2 does not present a comprehensive list of desired virtues in women's lives. Judging from other scriptural admonitions, much more can be taught. In fact, in order for a woman to be a capable teacher of other women, there are other qualities that would be helpful, and even necessary, in the disciplemaking task.

I am blessed to have resourceful comrades in discipleship who often provide feedback and input in a number of areas. I asked these group leaders this question: What character qualities are high priority for the disciplemaker? Each of them wrote down a number of qualities and when I compiled them, the list was impressive and somewhat daunting. It speaks well of these leaders who know what it takes to equip other women.

Desired Qualities in a Disciplemaker

Love for God and His Word
Open to the Holy Spirit's leading
Willing to invest in people
Committed to pray for disciples
Soft, teachable heart
Morally upright
Willing to sacrifice time and energy
Able to step out of one's comfort zone
Hospitable
Disciplined
A good listener
Humble
Aware of the culture
Has an established worldview
Able to keep group on track
Can balance structure and flexibility
Discerning
Teacher
Patient
A servant's heart
Caring
Diligent
Vulnerable
Sees the bigger picture
Trustworthy
Loving
Life-long learner
Others-centered
Passionate
Organized
Encourager
Approachable
Able to challenge
Obedient to Christ
Faithful

Willing to be an example even though imperfect
Integrity---what I teach, I believe, and it shows in my life

Added to the attributes in Titus 2, this makes for quite a roster of qualifications! If used to advertise for disciplers, no one would volunteer! What this list conveys is that working with others does require a diversity of character traits, not all at once, but over the course of time and study. What is stimulating to me is that these attributes truly make a woman beautiful. They are needed in many areas of life, and the disciplemaking endeavor can reinforce them in a woman or grow them from scratch.

Biblical Women of Influence

God has been faithful to women by giving them role models in His Word. Although the descriptions of these women are often brief (how we'd love to know more!), it is enough to know that throughout history God has placed women in positions of influence in order that His purposes could be accomplished. We can learn from observing some of the biblical archetypes in our Judeo-Christian heritage.

Sarah – Called the "Mother of Nations," she sojourned with her husband in a foreign land, was the victim of his lies but also the object of God's sovereign selection, and experienced a miraculous old-age birth. Greatly loved by Abraham, after her long life of 127 years, the entire chapter of Genesis 23 is given over to her burial. She is listed in the Hebrews 11 "Hall of Fame" chapter because "she considered Him faithful who had promised" (vs. 11).

Rebekah – A serving, hard-working beauty, she went hundreds of miles with a stranger to marry a stranger. A sobering example of manipulation, when God told her that two nations were in her womb and the older would serve the younger, she used her power and influence in the family to maneuver God's will to her liking.

Miriam – As a girl, she showed wisdom in guarding baby Moses, and as a woman, she was a brilliant, patriotic leader of the women of Israel. There is no record of her marriage. She played the timbrel, led the Hebrew women in singing and dancing, and wrote one of the earliest songs of Hebrew deliverance. When she spoke out against Moses publicly, she was stricken with leprosy and the encampment of Israel came to a standstill until she was healed. Like her brothers, Aaron and Moses, she did not reach the promised land, and when she died, her funeral was celebrated in a solemn manner for 30 days.

Deborah – A homemaker who gave counsel to people under a tree in front of her house, she became a much respected and sought-after advisor on political affairs. By common consent of the people, she was placed at the height of power as a judge and became a "Joan of Arc" to Israel. She denounced the lack of good male leadership and burned with indignation at the oppression of her people. When the fainthearted military leader, Barak, said to her, "If you will go with me, I will go; but if you won't go with me, I won't go" (Judges 4:8), she confidently encouraged him, and together they defeated Sisera and his charioteers. The fact that Israel was "at rest" for 40 years while she was a judge, attests to her wise leadership and strong character.

Ruth – Loveable and supportive of her mother-in-law, she submitted to the wishes of the older woman. Bold enough to approach Boaz while he slept, she risked her reputation while trusting Naomi, and in a customary manner, claimed Boaz's legal protection as a near kinsman of the family. After marrying Boaz, they had a son, Obed, and from him sprang the auspicious lineage of the House of David. Boaz, Ruth, Obed, Jesse and David are all mentioned in the genealogy of Jesus Christ in the first chapter of the New Testament.

Abigail – A capable and affluent woman, she was faithful to her husband Nabal in spite of his heavy drinking and reputation for being "churlish and evil in his doings" (I Sam. 25:3). A hospitable woman as well, she provided abundantly for their employees and guests. When Nabal refused supplies to the fugitive David and his 600 men (even though David had protected Nabal's herds), Abigail foresaw the impending disaster and bloodshed, and hastily prepared a huge amount of food, which she humbly delivered to David. When the sober Nabal learned from Abigail how close he had come to being slain by David, he became violently ill and died ten days later. David affectionately remembered Abigail, took her as his wife, and with their marriage, his life took on a higher purpose, destined to become the great king of Israel.

Esther – Reared by her cousin Mordecai, an official at the palace gate, Esther respected his advice and submitted to his encouragement to become the queen of King Ahasuerus. She took risks so a Jewess could be in the inner courts at a difficult time in Israel's history. Deeply distressed by the threat to annihilate her people, she saw her position as God-given "for such a time as this" (Esther 4:14). After prayer and fasting, she exercised great wisdom in approaching the king, and when authority was given her, she used it to protect the Jews by law and give them the freedom to kill their enemies.

Mary – Standing apart from other women in history, Mary has become the embodiment of all that is revered in womanhood. Art, music and literature throughout the ages have honored this woman who was called by Gabriel and Elizabeth, "blessed among women" (Luke 1:28, 42). Unique because of her part in the miracle of the virgin birth, she went from humble obscurity to worldwide adulation in the generations that succeeded her. Suffering much because of her unique privilege, her unshakeable belief in the providence of God, demonstrated by His faithfulness to Israel, sustained her throughout her life. She was grounded in the Old Testament scriptures and never faltered in her divine mission as the mother of the only begotten Son of God.

Mary and Martha – Close, personal friends of Jesus, their home was a respite for Him as well as a gathering place for conversation with others. Although Martha is portrayed as an assertive, practical and busy hostess, she uttered one of the most striking confessions of faith in the New Testament: "Lord, I believe that you are the Christ, the Son of God, who comes into the world" (John 11:27). Mary is remembered for her rapt attention at Jesus' feet, and later, anointing those feet with costly ointment. The two sisters stood by Jesus as He wept with grief over the death of their brother Lazarus, and their loving attitude was a stark contrast to the jealousy and hate of others standing by.

Lydia – A successful, influential businesswoman, she initiated gatherings at her home for the Apostle Paul. A strong female supporter of his, he obviously was comfortable and welcomed in her home. When Paul and Silas were released from prison in Philippi, they went immediately to Lydia's house where there was mutual encouragement among the believers.

Dorcas – Apparently a woman of affluence, Dorcas' home was a workshop where she established a service to many. Called a woman "full of good works" (Acts 9:36), she was benevolent, compassionate and devout. Because she so generously gave of herself to others, her name today is still synonymous with acts of charity. When she suddenly died, the people of Joppa could not imagine life without her and sent for the Apostle Peter. In the midst of their great grief and weeping, Peter was used by God to raise Dorcas from the dead, so she is one of the few humans in history who have had that experience.

Priscilla – A scholarly, influential woman who came out of Rome to live in Corinth and Ephesus, she was a teacher of the eloquent and learned Apollos. She and her husband, Aquila, were tentmakers, and it was with them that Paul worked the same trade in their home. The church assembled in her home, which was a rendezvous for many believers wanting to learn more about their newfound beliefs. Known for her hospitality, she influenced many through her gracious service and bright mind. Early historians attest to her fame by recording the deeds of "St. Prisca."

The Virtuous Woman – The "excellent wife" of Proverbs 31 is literature's most perfect picture of a woman whose "price is far above rubies" (vs. 10). The sheer beauty of a virtuous woman is detailed in this magnificent chapter, giving women everywhere a role model that is worthy of emulation. Her decorum, creativity, chastity, diligence, efficiency, business foresight, earnestness, and loyal love for her husband and children are brilliantly illuminated in this description. This ideal woman typifies almost all the admirable qualities traditionally associated with women, applicable to every generation, and she is a motivating force in all cultures and societies throughout the world. God, in His faithfulness to women, has given this mirror in which all women can examine themselves and find inspiration.

These Biblical examples are given here as a reminder that God has used women throughout the ages to influence others, from Dorcas in a personal domestic way, to Deborah and Esther on a national scale. Many other examples from the pages of history could be cited for their impact on communities and nations throughout the world. The common traits of these Biblical models include strength, leadership, creativity and compassion, which were obvious in their active involvement in people's lives. It is also obvious that they used their homes as places to affect others. That is a great tool in the life of the woman discipler.

USING THE HOME AS A PLACE OF MINISTRY

It is highly recommended that the woman discipler use her home as a gathering place for her group. Obviously, this cannot be done when disciplemaking is occurring at the "office," but whenever possible, the leader should have the women she is discipling in her home. There are several reasons for this.

1. THE HOME IS AN EXTENSION OF WHO YOU ARE.

Much is learned about a person by being in her home, so it facilitates an intimacy that a leader must have with her group. From the way the house is decorated to the way the family's schedule and activities are handled, all make known the personality and priorities of the discipler. And because no one is perfect, the home will not be perfect, and that is important to all involved. Electricity failures, a surprise flood in the basement, an emergency phone call as the women are walking in the door, remnants from a house guest, remodeling, painting, wallpapering, and a sick child home from school, are all part of family life. Although effort should always be taken to make the environment as conducive as possible for an uninterrupted special time together, these things will happen when meeting in a home. But if our discipling is going to be more than academic, then what better place can real life be modeled than in the home.

2. YOU CAN CONTROL THE ENVIRONMENT.

Except for unexpected circumstances which happen occasionally, the beauty of meeting in your own home is that you are in charge of the get-together. All the extra touches to create a warm atmosphere can be planned and prepared by the leader. The refreshments and how they are served are creatively determined by the hostess. The start and finish time of the meeting are in the leader's hands. Knowing that there will be a two-hour (or whatever) assembling of women in your home gives a special opportunity for the discipler to exercise leadership in the details of the environment as well as the meeting itself. The women are your guests and you are the hostess.

3. Variety can be exercised.

When a group gathers weekly in a restaurant or another public facility, it is the same room, the same décor, the same sounds, the same smells, the same utensils and the same atmosphere week after week. All of that can be varied when meeting in a home. Examples would be: having breakfast in the backyard; using antique teacups and a lace tablecloth at the dining room table; pulling chairs up close to the fireplace on a brisk winter morning; sitting at the kitchen table with the birdfeeder in view; varying the mugs and dishes used; sitting on the back deck with the autumn leaves floating downward; arranging chairs in a tight circle in the family room; frequently providing a variety of hot drinks (tea, coffee, cocoa, cider, and other exotic mixes); planning for protein as well as carbohydrates in the food; having appropriate music playing when the women enter (Christmas, Easter, Celtic, Gregorian chants, hymns, Bach, etc.); lighting candles on a dreary day, using pretty napkins, and having good smells from the oven greet the women as they enter. I've had women ask as they enter, "What room are we meeting in today?" It's fun to make each week a little unpredictable so the mundane is avoided.

4. The ordinary is hallowed.

There is something so common and ordinary about a home. The daily routine and duties, the comings and goings of the family members, the upkeep, the conversation and the familiar furnishings can all be taken for granted. With the pressure of the last few decades upon women to find fulfillment apart from the home, there has been a devaluation of the home itself…its importance and significance in society. Many homes (and families) today reek of neglect. Or the home and family are just taken for granted. In his wonderful little book, *Splendor in the Ordinary*, Thomas Howard speaks of recognizing the beauty in the commonplace because more is happening than meets the eye. As he moves from room to room in a typical home, he says it's finding joy in humble service, seeing the worth of each individual, learning lessons of love that lead to joy, and seeing the holy in the ordinary. On page 10, he states: "It is the argument of this book that we do, in fact, walk daily among the hallows...We have to recover the sense of the hallowed as being all around us. We will have to open our eyes and try to see once more the commonplace as both cloaking and revealing the holy to us. We will have to refuse resolutely the secularism that has made ordinariness unholy. We live in a dark age, and somewhere in this murk there have got to be lights burning in shrines and on altars, bearing witness to the presence of the holy."

This kind of splendor can be recognized and developed in any home if the "eye" sees more than the everyday routine. In addition to that, I believe that using our homes as places of ministry gives special significance to our house and family. Within our walls, wonderful dynamics occur with the fun, eating, serving, conversation, prayer, worship, study and interaction. It is a privilege to use the material things God has given us to encourage this kind of activity right where we live. Children growing up in such a home reap the rich benefits of such an environment. The home is much more than a showcase of furniture or a motel where people come at the end of the day. It is a place where God's all-encompassing love is demonstrated and experienced by those who enter. It is where He, Himself, meets with those who recognize His presence. This gives grandeur to the commonplace and nobility to all who live there.

5. All women need a home.

The Bible connects women with the home, and for good reason. When the sovereign Creator fashioned a woman out of man, the specific reason given in Genesis 2:18 was that she should be a "helper suitable to him." Eve made many things possible for Adam as a companion and co-worker. Household and family were also now a reality for him. God honored the woman by giving her the physical capabilities of bearing and sustaining the young, so she forever became intrinsically linked with the home. A high call and privilege, a woman functions best when she does not ignore the instincts within her that are satisfied and fulfilled in the home.

But history is replete with examples of women who have never married or mothered children, or because of the fall (disease, war, death, divorce), are living without the companionship of a husband. Does this exempt them from the need for a home? Do only married women get to nurture their "nesting" urges and longings and know what *home* really is? By no means. Because of the original design, no woman can afford to ignore what the Creator placed within. Too much is at stake. Her womanliness and femininity will be stunted if she discounts or disregards the inner longings unique to the female sex. In spite of the bountiful opportunities for women to succeed in arenas outside the home, she cannot treat as meaningless something that is freighted with meaning: her ancient and historical connection with the home. True feminine authenticity is discovered in this amphitheater of activity. The very substance of womanhood is developed and nourished in a *place* where creativity can be expressed…and expressed according to the individuality of the woman. From the décor, food, and cleaning styles to the rendering of service to others, the opportunities are limitless. The home is truly a place where a woman can "lose her life in order to find it."

Women just respond in a home environment. That's why discipling is effective in a home. Women react to the smells, sights and sounds of a home and it reaches their heart. That is why unmarried women need to be in a home, but also need to use their own place for the same. Whether it is a temporary dorm room, an apartment, mobile home or house, it is *home* for the time being and it can be used as a place of service and creativity. In fact, nothing makes a house a home like hospitality. So, no matter the stage in life… young single, newly married, small children, empty nester, older single, divorced, widowed, or older married…, a woman needs a home. And using the home as a place of ministry is one of the best ways to experience the authenticity that is so sought after in our present culture.

A recognition of all this can be a comfort and encouragement to women who have been heavily influenced by contemporary messages. In recent years, a great disservice has been handed to women in the drive to seek equality with men. "Equality" has been misunderstood to mean "same as," and imply everything from the equivalent in salary to physical endurance, ability, and verbal expression. Much grace and beauty, both in appearance and speech has been sacrificed in the scramble to be "one of the guys." If equality were understood in terms of human dignity and worth, much of the conversation would have been clarified and certainly shortened.

It is sad to see a woman profane the two areas that are such a vital part of her identity: her body and her home. (*Profane* meaning "to carelessly disregard what is meaningful.") Ignoring the important link between the female body and the person herself can lead to disillusionment. Disregarding the connection between the woman and the home can lead to endless searching for meaning. Instead of competing with men, a woman can learn to revel in the boundaries of her femininity, just as men have to live within the limits of their masculinity. One of the nicest services the sexes can offer each other is for each to accept their gender. Said another way, one of the nicest things a woman can do for a man is to be a woman.

The woman discipler has a significant privilege and opportunity to recapture the value of womanhood with those she teaches. Because disciplemaking is not a gender-neutral experience in academia, her teaching will be filtered through her femaleness, as it should be. As a person of influence, she can use all that is at her disposal to give credibility to her instruction: her walk with Christ, her knowledge of the Scriptures, her reliance on the Holy Spirit, her calling as a woman and the experiences born out of that, her education, her successes, her afflictions and her home are all part of her unique and significant journey. They make for quite a package. Being a disciple of Christ, and being a woman, opens the door for a rich life with limitless opportunities as an influencer of women.

CHAPTER XIII

FINAL THOUGHTS

Life is filled with potential for worthwhile commitments and fruitful involvements, and it easy to spread oneself too thin. In order to concentrate on a few people, a balanced course of action must be set. Paul referred to pressing toward the mark and finishing his course (Phil. 3:13-14; II Tim. 4:7), and it must have taken determination on his part not to get sidetracked by myriads of opportunities that no doubt came his way. When there is a willingness to work with a few people, it implies a single-minded approach to life. It requires a readiness to evaluate all opportunities in light of the primary goal.

Choosing Our Involvements

Personally, I believe there can be a great deal of variety in one's life while maintaining the goal of disciplemaking. In fact, it is good to balance a small group endeavor with other kinds of activities that are more broad-based, such as athletics, concerts, retreats, church gatherings, neighborhood parties, having people for dinner, etc. But if the prime objective in life is the training of a few, then there must be time for concentration on that goal. And it will mean graciously saying "no" to some things that really look attractive.

Some years ago, I realized that if I was going to be faithful and available to the women I worked with, I would have to be in town.

That meant limiting outside speaking engagements that not only took me away, but required valuable time in preparation. Because Tom and I have always lived away from our families, and now our married children are far from us, reserving time to visit family has to be a priority. Therefore, I can't be traveling to other places and traveling to visit family and expect to do a good job of discipling people. Because of our commitment to discipleship, both Tom and I have limited our outside speaking engagements. Even though saying "no" to some of these opportunities was difficult, the return on that kind of investment is low compared to the investment of disciplemaking

It takes wisdom to know where to expend our time and energy. When I've had to make a difficult choice on whether or not to commit to a new opportunity and there has been no clear direction from the Lord, Tom and I try to reach a decision by praying and thinking through the pros and cons. Sometimes, I submit the opportunity to women who know me well and have a feel for the women's ministry in our church. I've received prayerful support and wise counsel from these trusted friends. Even though these decisions could be classified as "personal," they really aren't. All of our decisions cause ripples, because we do not live isolated lives and make independent choices apart from people we love. The rippling result of our choices is very real. That's why we choose our involvements carefully.

Some years ago, I had to make a choice between continuing to lead our women's community Bible study and leading a discipleship group. As much as I enjoyed the women in this large study, and preparing for the weekly lecture, I knew I could not continue with that and devote time to discipleship. The decision was submitted for prayer and counsel. When about 12 of us met, clear direction was given to me to follow the Lord's leading into discipleship, but continue to lecture a few times each year at the continuing Bible study. That has worked well, and it enables me to retain contact with a fruitful ministry.

A Possessive Attitude

It has always been difficult for me to refer to the women in my group as "my disciples." That's because they really aren't, of course. I want them to be Christ's disciples, not mine. So I usually say, "women in my group," even though that gets old after awhile. There are a couple of things to consider here. Even though I have invited women to come into my group for an extended period of time, resulting in a closeness that I will not have with other women, I do not claim ownership in their lives. They are not *my* women, *my* girls or *my disciples*. I do not build a wall around them, refusing them input from anyone but me. This kind of possessive attitude is dangerous and certainly unscriptural. Even though Paul, Peter and John used endearing terms when writing their letters, such as "little children," "flock," "beloved bond servant," etc., they reminded these people that they belonged to Christ, not to the apostles.

On the other hand, Paul said repeatedly, "be imitators of me;" or "follow my example." Because he was a spiritual father to many, he did want those under his teaching to view him as their primary model. The Judaizers were a constant threat in distorting what he taught; therefore, he reminded people that he was their original teacher and desired their allegiance, not so he could possess them, but guard them from heresy. He had a protective love rather than a possessive motivation.

I've heard Christians say, "I don't want people to follow my example. I want them to follow Christ's example." That's the politically correct thing to say, of course, and it probably does reflect a humble spirit. But the truth of the matter is, people will follow your example whether you like it or not. To follow Christ or be an imitator of Paul is an abstract concept, especially when one is a new believer. It's difficult to relate to someone you've never seen and is far removed from you historically. If Biblical principles are to be caught, then they need to be taught by flesh-and-blood examples. This is perhaps one of the most sobering and humbling features of disciplemaking. The way I live my life really does matter because it *will* be an example for others to follow. I can't take people beyond where I am.

On the other hand, this is very motivating! It causes me to be a continuous learner myself, to read and study well, to be aware of weaknesses in my character and to be sensitive to the Holy Spirit's guidance each day. I am living life for more than just me. How I live it really does matter.

Child-raising is a good picture of this. A young child is dependent on his parents and imitates their behavior, speech, and ways of doing things quite naturally. Building on the foundation of the parents' example, he will include some variations as he gets older. The parents, meanwhile, learn the delicate balance of taking full responsibility for the nurturing of this child, yet holding him in an open hand, knowing that he really isn't theirs. He is God's child, loaned to them for their guidance and input, and someday, he will be released to do what God wants him to do. Parents who are possessive of their children actually stifle their children's growth and create an unhealthy dependency.

So it is in discipling others. When there is a close relationship that involves intimacy, nurturing, encouragement, care and concern, there is a real sense of protection on the part of the discipler. All of this is necessary and good. The temptation, of course, is to get possessive. Those in our care really belong to the Lord and He can use others to strengthen and affirm what we have been teaching. So we care deeply and try to do our best at nurturing, but hold those we love in an open hand.

THE 3-PRONGED ASPIRATION

In his book, *Personal Disciplemaking* (chapter 3), Christopher Adsit relates a 3-stage process in teaching others to observe what Christ commanded. It is practical and easy to remember, so I recommend it here with some additional comments. The three "L's" are *learn it, love it,* and *live it.*

1. LEARN IT

This involves the intellect and acquiring a head knowledge of what is taught. There needs to be content first of all. The Bible is the primary textbook in discipleship, of course, but other materials can be carefully chosen and used to give the information needed to establish the framework in which the learning takes place. Teaching needs to be orderly and systematic so there is a flow to the material being digested. In order that those in the group may "learn it," the discipler spends much time preparing the content.

Most Christians are short on content and heavy on application. The information is scant, and the desire is to talk about how it applies to *us*. This is a bad habit that is common in the evangelical world, and it accommodates the cultural norms of sound-byte information, anemic dialogue and self-centered living. When people begin making applications prematurely, the learning stops. No one needs to think anymore because, after all, this is how it's applied. If one of our goals as disciplers is to re-establish the collective Christian mind, then we need to begin with the few in our charge. Many Christians do not recognize how unthinking they are or how experienced-centered their walk is. Just listening to them talk is a clue: "I feel" is the term most often used when expressing their faith. "I believe" or "I know" is infrequently used. So we must encourage thinking, especially if we want believers to form strong convictions.

Biblical illiteracy is high today, and if most evangelicals took a basic theology test, the average score would probably be worse than failing. Having had 40 years of work within the evangelical church, Tom and I are always amazed at what Christians *don't* know, even after having been in the church for years. Discipleship groups are a perfect place to turn this around. It is vitally important that the intellect be stirred with good content. So the first step is to *learn it*.

2. Love It

After acquiring a head knowledge, the second stage would be gaining a heart knowledge. This comes when the truth "hits home," convictions are formed and the emotions get involved. There is a deep stirring within as one begins to grasp the absolute wonder of the Christian faith.

Having grown up in a home and church where the Bible was emphasized, I was familiar with Christian terminology and the fundamentals of the faith. I knew I loved Jesus. I did not know I could "fall in love" with my beliefs. That happened in Theology 101 class with Dr. Charles Horne at the Moody Bible Institute. His lectures were designed to give content, not necessarily stir the emotions, so I was surprised at my reaction to his teaching. For the first time, I was challenged to consider whether or not God really existed. Having never opened my mind to that before, when I pondered the evidence for His existence over a period of weeks, I was deeply moved by my conclusion that He really was there, and that He had revealed Himself. During the Soteriology section of that class as we were studying the facets of our salvation, Dr. Horne's lectures on God's grace impacted me to the point that I was literally dazed by what I had learned. I could not wrap my mind around God's grace. It was huge and beyond my comprehension. Grace really was "amazing" and at the very core of God's actions. One day after class, I sought the solitude of my dorm room, knelt by my bed and wept with unspeakable gratitude for what God had done in spite of my undeserving state. I began to love my beliefs, and knew I would forever be loyal to them.

This kind of love is motivational. There is an eagerness to learn more, and to learn it in such a way that it can be shared. This is when the "light bulbs go on" and an excitement stirs within because of the truth learned. So, the second stage is when the head knowledge travels to the heart, and the response is: "I love it!"

3. Live it

Chris Adsit likens this to "hand knowledge." The learning now becomes action. This is the personal fruitfulness which is naturally born out of the knowing. True conviction will find its way into life application. As an example, when I first began to grasp what is meant by being created in the image of God, I knew I was on to something fundamental and critical to my worldview. Recognizing the value and worth of *all* humans because they are *all* image-bearers of God, not just those who profess Christ, affected my willingness to spend time with non-Christians. Without making them a project, I could now enjoy conversation and times together, whether or not they ever became believers. They were worth spending time with because of their inherent worth as humans. I loved this new awareness of the dignity of mankind and it changed the way I related to non-believing neighbors as well as to Christians.

So, loving what is learned will have practical application. It makes one want to live it.

How Intense Do We Get?

Because I have never felt that enough was enough with any of my groups, I have pondered the issue of intensity and wondered if more could be done. There always seems to be a feeling of incompletion when a group comes to the end of its designated time together (in my case, 1½-2 years), having covered the syllabus, and the notebook is full. Part of that is due to the material itself and the fact that only so much time can be spent on areas that are potentially huge. For instance, how much time does a group spend on church history? What periods do you cover? When you open that door, how far in do you go? I've often viewed the discipleship material as a teaser to whet the appetite for more. There always is much more that can be studied in any area of theology. Knowing how to abbreviate the areas without having a stunted effect is challenging.

Another contributing factor to the feeling of incompletion is the development of relationships. The women have gotten comfortable with each other and they like being together. They know a lot more about each other than at the beginning, and it seems right that it should continue. Abruptly coming to a halt almost seems cruel. Just when the relationships are getting good we have to call it quits. (For that reason, some of my groups have "weaned" themselves off each other by going from weekly meetings to monthly meetings after our time is completed.)

And when is the discipler really finished discipling a person? Even though the "formal" time has concluded, does that mean that everyone is where they need to be? People usually want more. Does discipling a person ever really end? It doesn't seem so.

I do not think there are pat answers to these questions. They are the challenges in disciplemaking that keep us on our toes and assessing what we are doing. Having been in a discipling relationship with someone will always impact that friendship, and in a sense, the discipling never stops. Probably one of my greatest frustrations is not being able to meet regularly with former group members. There are reunions and meetings for those who are presently leading groups, but having the time to sit and chat one-on-one would be so satisfying.

Tom and I have been to Wittenburg, Germany, a number of times, and whenever we are in Martin Luther's house, which has been beautifully restored, we are impressed with the fact that his students lived with him, sometimes for three years. His wife Katie would serve dinner to all of them as they sat around the table and continued their discussions (from which the book, *Tabletalk* originated). That's intensity! It sounds so ideal and much more thorough than what can happen with a once-a-week arrangement.

I have lamented not being able to do more with the individual women in my group apart from that weekly meeting. We do meet for lunch and other occasions, but it never seems to be enough. That is one of the primary reasons why I cannot have more than four women in my group. It is very difficult to spend valuable time with each one of them. That is why a discipler who travels a lot and is in and out of town will have trouble with the consistency factor of disciplemaking. She can lead a group, but there will have to be an understanding of the degree to which the group can be taken. Walt Henrichson says it well in *Disciples Are Made Not Born* (Chap. 12), where he likens this to a comfortable marriage where there is a lifestyle of freedom to travel, dine out, take vacations, and live in a beautiful home. The marriage becomes costly when it focuses on reproduction. Having children will limit some of those freedoms. Children are the difference between a comfortable and costly marriage. He says: "The difference between comfortable Christianity and costly Christianity is spiritual reproduction. It costs to become involved in the lives of people."

But is there a greater joy than having children? Words are inadequate to express the richness they add to a marriage. So much is learned by having children. So much is gained. And with spiritual reproduction, it is the same. Yes, it costs, but nurturing others is the best way to do life. The rewards far outweigh the costs. In part, it is realizing that in "losing one's life, one finds it."

The decision to reproduce is the right decision, and each of us must do the best we can with the resources the Lord has given us. I have learned to accept my limitations as I've matured, knowing that I cannot meet everyone's expectations. Being human is wonderful, but it does mean I must live within the boundaries of my limitedness, and contrary to current lingo, I can't have it all. If I choose to do certain things, it means I will choose not to do other things. We will not always achieve proper balance in all of life's responsibilities and privileges but we can still know the joy of being "workers together with the Lord." What we do will never be perfect, and it will probably feel incomplete, but in spite of that, life is rich and full, and we gladly participate in all the goodness that God has given.

APPENDIX - **THE CURRICULUM**

For the discipler who uses the Bible as the main textbook, any variety of materials can aid sound instruction. Because the discipling process needs to be orderly with a goal in view, thoughtful attention must be given to the content that will be covered. For this reason, a primary concern of a discipleship leader is the course of study that will be used during the discipling process.

Throughout this book, references are made to the curriculum which Judy has developed over the years. It is not included here because it is in the format of a loose-leaf binder; however, it is available for those desiring to pursue such a course.

The manual is designed to guide the leader in the weekly preparation for her group. Each member of the discipleship group begins with an empty 3-ringed binder. Only material for the current lesson is handed out. The pages grow week by week as the units are covered, therefore, each person is building a curriculum that will be used when the discipleship process is reproduced.

The syllabus for the curriculum is included here. The order of the outline is intended to cover basic doctrine before dealing with family and culture issues. Spiritual warfare, evangelism, gifts and calling seem to be a natural outflow after studying the church, family and culture, so they are organized accordingly.

The encouragement is to begin with doctrine because it provides the basis for discussion on any other subject. The outline does not provide all the points covered in each unit. It is basically a sketch of the possibilities within each category that can be adjusted to each group. Depending on the discipleship group, some units will become bigger or smaller than depicted in the syllabus. The outline merely gives an overview of the material that will be studied.

For information on obtaining the curriculum, please contact:

Women's Ministries	Phone: 317-873-4948
Zionsville Fellowship Church	Fax: 317-873-5008
9090 East State Road 334	www.zionsvillefellowship.org
Zionsville, IN 46077	

Prerequisites for obtaining the curriculum manual:

- ✧ The local church leadership must be in agreement that this curriculum will be used in the discipleship ministry of the church.
- ✧ People who will lead discipleship groups must be trained in the material. Judy and her coworkers are available to work with women desirous of leading groups.
- ✧ There should be a commitment by those involved to reproduce the discipling process.

SYLLABUS

I. **DISCIPLESHIP**

    A. Understanding the definition
    B. Knowing the goal and process
    C. Discussion of materials read

II. **KNOWING GOD THE FATHER**

    A. His character and nature
    B. His attributes and triunity
    C. Apologetics

III. **BEING HUMAN**

    A. Made in the image of God
    B. Creation mandates
    C. Maleness and femaleness
    D. Apologetics

IV. **WHO IS GOD THE SON?**

    A. His eternality
    B. His divinity
    C. His humanity
    D. Apologetics

V. **SALVATION**

    A. Formulate own testimony
    B. Sin and guilt
    C. Understanding God's forgiveness
    D. Understanding imputed righteousness and our position in Christ
    E. Apologetics

VI. **THE HOLY SPIRIT**

    A. Person and work
    B. Filling and walking
    C. Apologetcs

VII. **KNOWING THE SCRIPTURES**

    A. Authenticity of the Bible
    B. Historicity and the Canon
    C. Books and categories
    D. Means of reading, study and memorization
    E. Apologetics

VIII. **PRAYER**

    A. Ingredients of prayer
    B. Nature and necessity
    C. Apologetics

IX. **THE CHURCH**

    A. Scriptural portrayal
    B. Authority and community
    C. Church history
    D. Apologetics

X. **THE FAMILY**

    A. Microcosm of the church
    B. Family ingredients and purpose
    C. Understanding Biblical principles for marriage and children
    D. Apologetics

XI. **THE CULTURE**

    A. The "isms" of our age
    B. The present world spirit
    C. The balance between building and battle
    D. Real and practical involvements

XII. **SPIRITUAL WARFARE**

    A. Cults and world religions
    B. Satan-awareness

XIII. **EVANGELISM**

    A. Mission
    B. Methods of telling
    C. Leading a person to faith in Christ

XIV. **GIFTS AND CALLING**

    A. Spiritual gifts
    B. Calling
    C. Discerning God's will
    D. Discipleship

Printed in the United States
128479LV00002B/297/A